SCHOLASTIC

LITERACY PLACE

IT WORKS...AND KIDS LIKE IT!

SCHOLASTIC

SCHOLASTIC
LITERACY PLACE

IT WORKS...AND KIDS LIKE IT!

Manageable Instructional Plans

Literacy Place follows a clear, consistent pattern of instruction and provides support for all learners. The Teacher's Edition includes explicit skills instruction and integrates the language arts.

The Strongest System for Beginning Readers

Literacy Place provides direct instruction in phonics and phonological awareness and fully reflects current and confirmed research.

Assessment Tools to Monitor and Modify Instruction

Literacy Place features focused assessment that informs instruction and measures progress. The program offers strategies targeting students who need skills intervention, language-development support, and enrichment.

Power and Confidence for the Information Age

Literacy Place uses technology as an integral part of learning while connecting the classroom to the real world.

The Matrix

PERSONAL LITERACY	INTELLECTUAL LITERACY	SOCIAL LITERACY
Personal Voice	**Problem Solving**	**Teamwork**
We communicate in our unique voices as we grow and learn.	People have the power to solve problems.	Successful teams depend on the collaboration of individuals.

K

Stories About Us

Big Idea We listen to, tell, and create stories.
Mentor Grandmother: *Honey Wada*
Place Storytelling Corner
Project "All About Me" Class Book

See It, Solve It

Big Idea We see problems and find solutions.
Mentor Clay Animator: *Becky Wible*
Place Claymator's Studio
Project Dramatization

All Together Now!

Big Idea We share and help each other.
Mentor Pizza Maker: *Kwaku Twumasi*
Place Restaurant
Project Big Book of Menus

1

Hello!

Big Idea We share what we like.
Mentor Author: *Donald Crews*
Place Writer's Home
Project Scrapbook

Problem Patrol

Big Idea There are many kinds of problems.
Mentor Veterinarian: *Fay Vittetoe*
Place Veterinarian's Office
Project Pet Care Guide

Team Spirit

Big Idea It's fun to do things together.
Mentor Soccer Coach: *Danny Prenat*
Place Soccer Stadium
Project Game Rule Book

2

Snapshots

Big Idea Our actions tell about us.
Mentor Photographer: *Bruce Thorson*
Place Sports Arena
Project Exhibit

Super Solvers

Big Idea There may be more than one way to solve a problem.
Mentor Toy Designer: *Mary Rodas*
Place Toy Company
Project Safety Poster Campaign

Lights! Camera! Action!

Big Idea Creative teams produce great performances.
Mentor Theater Director: *Judith Martin*
Place Children's Theater
Project Play Production

3

What's New?

Big Idea We learn about our world through new experiences.
Mentor Wilderness Guide: *Keith Jardine*
Place Wilderness School
Project Anecdote

Big Plans

Big Idea Making and using plans can help us solve problems.
Mentor Architect: *Jack Catlin*
Place Construction Site
Project Floor Plan

On the Job

Big Idea Teams work best when they use each member's strengths to get the job done.
Mentor Art Director: *Max Jerome*
Place Ad Agency
Project Ad Campaign

4

Chapter by Chapter

Big Idea We are always adding to our life story.
Mentor Author: *Jerry Spinelli*
Place Bookstore
Project Personal Narrative

What an Idea!

Big Idea People solve problems by inventing new things.
Mentor Inventor: *Julie Lewis*
Place Inventor's Office
Project Invention Marketing Plan

Discovery Teams

Big Idea When we work as a team, we learn new things about our world.
Mentor Astronaut: *Dr. Mae Jemison*
Place Space Center
Project Multimedia Presentation

5

Making a Difference

Big Idea Each of us is inspired by the lives of others.
Mentor Musician: *Joseph Shabalala*
Place Concert Hall
Project Tribute

It's a Mystery

Big Idea We can solve mysteries using reason, logic, and intuition.
Mentor Forensic Chemist: *Lilly Gallman*
Place Detective Headquarters
Project Investigative Report

Voyagers

Big Idea We depend on a network of people when we explore.
Mentor Travel Agent: *Marie French*
Place Travel Agency
Project Travel Magazine

PERSONAL LITERACY	INTELLECTUAL LITERACY	SOCIAL LITERACY

Creative Expression
People express themselves in many creative ways.

Managing Information
Finding and using information helps us live in our world.

Community Involvement
Communities are built on the contributions of the people who live there.

Express Yourself

Big Idea We express ourselves through songs, sounds, stories, dance, and art.
Mentor Author: *Pat Mora*
Place Author's Studio
Project Storybook

I Spy!

Big Idea Information is all around us.
Mentor Farmer: *Steven Powell*
Place Gardening Center
Project Garden Journal

Join In!

Big Idea We help our community.
Mentor Singer/Songwriter: *Tom Chapin*
Place Performance Stage
Project Community Sing

Imagine That!

Big Idea Imagination lets us look at things in new ways.
Mentor Muralist: *William Walsh*
Place Artist's Studio
Project Story Mural

Information Finders

Big Idea Information comes from many sources.
Mentor Marine Biologist: *Laela Sayigh*
Place Aquarium
Project Big Book of Information

Home Towns

Big Idea We are all members of a community.
Mentor Mayor: *Steve Yamashiro*
Place Mayor's Office
Project Visitor's Map

Story Studio

Big Idea People express themselves through stories and pictures.
Mentor Author & Artist: *Tomie dePaola*
Place Author's Studio
Project Picture Book

Animal World

Big Idea We use information to understand the interdependence of people and animals.
Mentor Zoo Curator: *Lisa Stevens*
Place Zoo
Project Zoo Brochure

Lend a Hand

Big Idea People can make a difference in their communities.
Mentor Police Officer: *Nadine Jojola*
Place Police Station
Project Community Expo

Hit Series

Big Idea A creative idea can grow into a series.
Mentor Author & Illustrator: *Joanna Cole & Bruce Degen*
Place Publishing Company
Project New Episode

Time Detectives

Big Idea Finding information in stories and artifacts brings the past to life.
Mentor Archaeologist: *Dr. Ruben Mendoza*
Place Archaeological Site
Project Time Capsule

Community Quilt

Big Idea In a community, some things continue and some things change.
Mentor Community Garden Director: *Lorka Muñoz*
Place Community Garden
Project Community Quilt

The Funny Side

Big Idea Sometimes humor is the best way to communicate.
Mentor Cartoonist: *Robb Armstrong*
Place Cartoonist's Studio
Project Comic Strip

Nature Guides

Big Idea Gathering and using information help us understand and describe the natural world.
Mentor Park Ranger: *Veronica Gonzales-Vest*
Place National Park Headquarters
Project Field Guide

It Takes a Leader

Big Idea In every community there are people who inspire others to take action.
Mentor Editor: *Suki Cheong*
Place Newspaper Office
Project Op-Ed Page

In the Spotlight

Big Idea We use our creativity to reach an audience.
Mentor Drama Coach: *José García*
Place Actor's Workshop
Project Stage Presentation

America's Journal

Big Idea Considering different points of view gives us a fuller understanding of history.
Mentor Historian/Author: *Russell Freedman*
Place Historical Museum
Project Historical Account

Cityscapes

Big Idea Cities depend on the strengths and skills of the people who live and work there.
Mentor Urban Planner: *Karen Heit*
Place Urban Planner's Office
Project Action Plan

Components

Pupil's Editions & Teacher's Editions

Literacy Place Kindergarten
provides a rich learning environment
including Big Books, Read Alouds,
Sentence Strips, Audiocassettes, Phonics
Manipulatives, Workbooks, Teacher
Editions, and much more.

Grades 1-5
▶ Literacy Place brings you what you would
expect from Scholastic—authentic, award-
winning children's literature.

▶ Our Teacher's Editions are easy to use, and
provide explicit skills instruction.

▶ You'll also find a management CD-ROM to
help you customize instruction to state and
district standards.

scholastic.com
Check it out! You'll find a
wealth of professional
support resources, plus a
lot of great stuff for kids
and parents.

Pupil's Editions   **Teacher's Editions**

Support Materials

Practice Literacy Place includes comprehensive practice resources.

✔ My Reading Workbook (1)
✔ Workshop and Project Cards (K-2)
✔ Practice Books (1-5)
✔ Spelling Resource Book (1-5)
✔ Grammar Resource Book (1-5)
✔ Handwriting Practice Book (K-3)
✔ ESL/ELD Resource Book (K-5)
✔ Skills Overhead Transparencies (2-5)
✔ Vocabulary Overhead Transparencies (2-5)
✔ Place Cards (3-5)

Assessment Literacy Place provides a wide range of assessment and evaluation options. (K-5)

✔ Placement Tests
✔ Assessment Handbook
✔ Classroom Management Forms
✔ Selection Tests (for every story!)
✔ Unit Tests (Forms A and B)
✔ Oral Reading Assessment
✔ Scholastic Reading Inventory
✔ TAAS Preparation and Practice Book
✔ Assessment System CD-ROM

Technology We set the industry standard.

✔ Phonics Practice CD-ROM (K-2)
✔ WiggleWorks Plus CD-ROM (K-2)
✔ Smart Place CD-ROM (3-5)
✔ Scholastic Management Suite (K-5)
✔ Staff Development Videos (K-5)
✔ Meet the Mentor Videos (K-5)
✔ Scholastic Network (K-5)
✔ Selection Audiocassettes (1-5)
✔ Classroom Resources CD-ROM (K-5)

Scholastic Solutions Only Scholastic can offer you the diverse range of materials you need for your classroom. Please call 1-800-Scholastic for a catalog. Ask about these exciting products:

✔ High-Frequency Readers (K-1)
✔ Sound and Letter Books (K-1)
✔ Big Books/Little Books (K-2)
✔ Phonemic Awareness Kit (K-2)
✔ Phonics Readers (K-3)
✔ Phonics Chapter Books (1-3)
✔ Phonics Workbooks (K-2)

✔ Guided Reading Program (K-5)
✔ Bilingual Support (K-5)
✔ Solares (K-5)
✔ Transition Program (3-6)
✔ Sprint Plus Intervention (3-6)
✔ READ 180 (4-8)
✔ Reading Counts! (K-8)

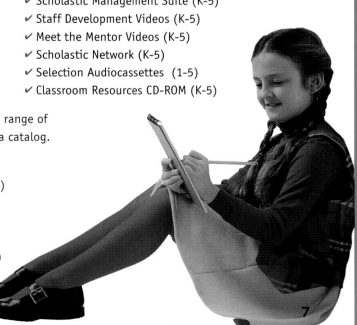

Advisors

Program Consultants

SKILLS, STRATEGIES, INSTRUCTION
James Bauman
Professor, University of Georgia,
Athens, Georgia

PHONICS AND EARLY READING
Wiley Blevins
Consultant and Educational Writer
New York, New York

ESL/ELD
Jacqueline Kiraithe-Cordova
Professor, California State, California

STAFF DEVELOPMENT
Nancy Cummings
Western Director of Implementation
Success For All School Restructuring
Phoenix, Arizona

BILINGUAL EDUCATION
James Cummins
Professor, Ontario Institute for
Studies in Education
Ontario, Canada

EARLY LITERACY DEVELOPMENT
Nell K. Duke
Michigan State University

ASSESSMENT/WRITING
Adele Fiderer
Consultant and Educational Writer
Scarsdale, New York

HANDWRITING
Steve Graham
Professor, University of Maryland
College Park, Maryland

WRITING
Shelley Harwayne
Director of Manhattan New School
New York, New York

SPELLING
Richard E. Hodges
Professor, University of Puget Sound
Tacoma, Washington

SPELLING
Louisa Moats
County Office of Education
Sacramento, California

VOCABULARY
William E. Nagy
Assistant Professor, University of Illinois
Champaign-Urbana, Illinois

FLEXIBLE GROUPING
Michael Opitz
Professor, University of Colorado
Boulder, Colorado

ESL/ELD
Robert Parker
Consultant, Brown University
Providence, Rhode Island

ESL/ELD
Cao Anh Quan
ESOL Program Specialist
Tallahassee, Florida

ESL/ELD
Kim Quan Nguyen-Lam
California State University
Long Beach, California

WRITING
Michael Strickland
Author, Consultant
Orange, New Jersey

Teacher Reviewers

Kim Andrews
Fourth Grade Reviewer
Baltimore, Maryland

Shirley Beard
Fourth Grade Reviewer
El Paso, Texas

Barbara Bloom
Fifth Grade Reviewer
Wall Lake, Iowa

Sherry Brown
Third Grade Reviewer
Georgetown, Texas

Lisa Buchholz
First Grade Reviewer
Wheaton, Illinois

Kathy Burdick
Fifth Grade Reviewer
Austin, Texas

Marianne Chorba
Fourth Grade Reviewer
Baltimore, Maryland

Peggy Colley
Third Grade Reviewer
Rocky Face, Georgia

Carol Curry
Third Grade Reviewer
Tallahassee, Florida

Claire Dale
First Grade Reviewer
National City, California

Mildred DeStefano
First Grade Reviewer
Brooklyn, New York

Doris Dillan
Grade Two Reviewer
San Jose, California

Oneaster Drummer
First Grade Reviewer
Cincinnati, Ohio

Ethel Durham
Third Grade Reviewer
Grand Rapids, Michigan

Patty Ernst
Second Grade Reviewer
Naples, New York

Alzada Fowler
First Grade Reviewer
Lake Helen, Florida

Jane Ginn
First Grade Reviewer
Rohnert Park, California

Amy Gordon
Third Grade Reviewer
New City, New York

Janet Gray
Fourth Grade Reviewer
Lake Helen, Florida

Velma Gunn
Fourth Grade Reviewer
New Rochelle, New York

Annie Ruth Harris
Third Grade Reviewer
Decatur, Alabama

Barbara Ann Hawkins
Second Grade Reviewer
Hamer, South Carolina

Amy Hom
Second Grade Reviewer
New York, New York

Min Hong
First Grade Reviewer
Brooklyn, New York

Susan Howe
Third Grade Reviewer
Ellicott City, Maryland

Barbara Jansz
First Grade Reviewer
Naperville, Illinois

Michele Jessen
First Grade Reviewer
El Paso, Texas

Ellen W. Johnson
Second Grade Reviewer
Chalfont, Pennsylvania

Vera Johnson
First Grade Reviewer
Uniondale, New York

Carol Kaiser
Third Grade Reviewer
Los Angeles, California

Karen Kolsky
Third Grade Reviewer
Philadelphia, Pennsylvania

Judy Keyak
Second Grade Reviewer
St. Petersburg, Florida

Jacqueline Krass
Second Grade Reviewer
Gulfport, Mississippi

Warren Livesley
Fourth Grade Reviewer
New York, New York

Libby Lesley
First Grade Reviewer
San Angelo, Texas

Dora I. Magana
Fourth Grade Reviewer
El Paso, Texas

Tim Mason
Second Grade Reviewer
Willington Florida

Carol Mercer
Fourth Grade Reviewer
National City, California

Betty Milburn
Third Grade Reviewer
Grand Prairie, Texas

Jane Moore
Third Grade Reviewer
Dallas, Texas

Sandy Nolan
Third Grade Reviewer
Salem, Wisconsin

Carol Ochs
Fifth Grade Reviewer
Noble, Oklahoma

Lynn Olson
Fifth Grade Reviewer
Omaha, Nebraska

Cynthia Orange
Second Grade Reviewer
Bronx, New York

Sue Panek
Fourth Grade Reviewer
Hawthorne, New Jersey

Deborah Peale
Fourth Grade Reviewer
Miami, Florida

Arturo Perez
Second Grade Reviewer
Ventura, California

Jeanette Reber
First Grade Reviewer
Rock Hill, South Carolina

Charlene Richardson
Fourth Grade Reviewer
Everett, Washington

Daria Rigney
Fifth Grade Reviewer
Brooklyn, New York

Andrea Ruff
First Grade Reviewer
Brooklyn, New York

Carol Shirmang
First Grade Reviewer
Palatine, Illinois

Wendy Smiley
Fourth Grade Reviewer
Syracuse, New York

Barbara Solomon
Second Grade Reviewer
Hempstead, New York

Alicia Sparkman
First Grade Reviewer
Plant City, Florida

Elaine Steinberg
Third Grade Reviewer
Fresh Meadows, New York

Bobby Stern
Third Grade Reviewer
Winston-Salem, North Carolina

Laura Stewart
First Grade Reviewer

Kate Taylor
Fifth Grade Reviewer
Baltimore, Maryland

Vasilika Terss
Second Grade Reviewer
St. Louis, Missouri

Linda Thorn
Fifth Grade Reviewer
Cranford, New Jersey

Gayle Thurn
Second Grade Reviewer
Piedmont, South Carolina

Jerry Trotter
Fifth Grade Reviewer
Chicago, Illinois

Julia Tucker
First Grade Reviewer
Hampton, Virginia

Patricia Viales
First Grade Reviewer
Salinas, California

Janielle Wagstaff
Second Grade Reviewer
Salt Lake City, Utah

Gail Weber
Fourth Grade Reviewer
Sherman Oaks, California

Elizabeth White
First Grade Reviewer
Bronx, New York

Karla Hawkins-Windeline
Second Grade Reviewer
Hickman, Nebraska

National Advisory Council

Barbara R. Foorman, Ph. D.
Professor of Pediatrics
Director of the Center for
Academic and Reading Skills
Houston, TX

Dr. Wilmer Cody
Commissioner of Education
Kentucky State Department
of Education
Frankfort, KY

Ms. Judy Mountjoy
Vice President
The National PTA
Chicago, IL

Ms. Anne Bryant
Executive Director
National School Boards
Association
Alexandria, VA

Dr. Anthony Alvarado
Chancellor for Instruction
San Diego City Schools
San Diego, CA

TEACHER'S EDITION

SCHOLASTIC

LITERACY PLACE®

UNIT 4

Express Yourself

LITERACY PLACE AUTHORS

CATHY COLLINS BLOCK
Professor, Curriculum and Instruction, Texas Christian University

LINDA B. GAMBRELL
Professor, Education, University of Maryland at College Park

VIRGINIA HAMILTON
Children's Author; Winner of the Newbery Medal, the Coretta Scott King Award and the Laura Ingalls Wilder Lifetime Achievement Award

DOUGLAS K. HARTMAN
Associate Professor of Language and Literacy, University of Pittsburgh

TED S. HASSELBRING
Co-Director of the Learning Technology Center and Professor in the Department of Special Education at Peabody College, Vanderbilt University

ADRIA KLEIN
Professor, Reading and Teacher Education, California State University at San Bernardino

HILDA MEDRANO
Dean, College of Education, University of Texas-Pan American

GAY SU PINNELL
Professor, School of Teaching and Learning, College of Education, Ohio State University

D. RAY REUTZEL
Provost/Academic Vice President, Southern Utah University

DAVID ROSE
Founder and Executive Director of the Center for Applied Special Technology (CAST); Lecturer, Harvard University Graduate School of Education

ALFREDO SCHIFINI
Professor, School of Education, Division of Curriculum Instruction, California State University, Los Angeles

DELORES STUBBLEFIELD SEAMSTER
Principal, N.W. Harllee Elementary, Dallas, Texas; Consultant on Effective Programs for Urban Inner City Schools

QUALITY QUINN SHARP
Author and Teacher-Educator, Austin, Texas

JOHN SHEFELBINE
Professor, Language and Literacy Education, California State University at Sacramento

GWENDOLYN Y. TURNER
Associate Professor of Literacy Education, University of Missouri at St. Louis

Acknowledgments and credits appear on pages R28–R29, which constitute an extension of this copyright page.
Copyright © 2000 by Scholastic Inc.   All rights reserved.   Published by Scholastic Inc.   Printed in the U.S.A.
ISBN 0-439-07880-6 (National)
SCHOLASTIC, SCHOLASTIC LITERACY PLACE, and associated logos and designs are trademarks and/or registered trademarks of Scholastic Inc.
3 4 5 6 7 8 9 10   14   07 06 05 04 03 02 01 00

TABLE OF CONTENTS

Express Yourself

We express ourselves through songs, sounds, stories, dance, and art.

What's in Front?

What's in Back?

WEEKS 1 AND 2

WEEK 1

WEEK 2

WEEKS 3 AND 4

WEEK 3

WEEK 4

WEEKS 5 AND 6

WEEK 5

WEEK 6

Kindergarten Place at a Glance

 PHONOLOGICAL AWARENESS
ABC Song, Names,
Alphabetic Knowledge

A Was Once an Apple Pie
by Edward Lear

- **Mentor:** Honey Wada,
  a grandmother
- **Place:** Storytelling Corner

PHONOLOGICAL AWARENESS PHONICS

A B C D E F

Apples, Alligators and also Alphabets
by Odette and Bruce Johnson

- **Mentor:** Becky Wible,
  a claymator
- **Place:** Claymator's Studio

PHONOLOGICAL AWARENESS PHONICS

G H I J K L

Eating the Alphabet: Fruits and Vegetables from A to Z
by Lois Ehlert

- **Mentor:** Kwaku Twumasi,
  a pizza chef
- **Place:** Restaurant

CREATIVE EXPRESSION

Express Yourself
We express ourselves through songs, sounds, stories, dance, and art.

WEEKS 1 AND 2
 Listen to the Desert
by Pat Mora

A-Hunting We Will Go!
by Steven Kellogg

Mouse Mess
by Linnea Riley

 WIGGLEWORKS PLUS:
Let's Get the Rhythm

WEEKS 3 AND 4
 The Itsy Bitsy Spider
by Iza Trapani

The Three Little Pigs
by Gavin Bishop

Mama Zooms
by Jane Cowen-Fletcher

 WIGGLEWORKS PLUS:
Clifford the Big Red Dog

WEEKS 5 AND 6
 Good-Night, Owl!
by Pat Hutchins

Minerva Louise at School
by Janet Morgan Stoeke

Whistle for Willie
by Ezra Jack Keats

········ STORYTELLING ········
The Spider Weaver

MANAGING INFORMATION

I Spy!
Information is all around us.

WEEKS 1 AND 2
 Nature Spy
by Shelley Rotner and
Ken Kreisler

Mice Squeak, We Speak
by Tomie dePaola

What Joe Saw
by Anna Grossnickle Hines

········ STORYTELLING ········
The Coyote and the Turtle

WEEKS 3 AND 4
 From Head to Toe
by Eric Carle

Over on the Farm
by Christopher Gunson

Foal
photographed by Gordon Clayton

 WIGGLEWORKS PLUS:
A Tree Can Be...

WEEKS 5 AND 6
 Flower Garden
by Eve Bunting

I Am the Peach
by Luisa de Noriega

The Tale of Peter Rabbit
by Beatrix Potter

 WIGGLEWORKS PLUS: **My Garden**

COMMUNITY INVOLVEMENT

Join In!
We help our community.

WEEKS 1 AND 2
 My River
by Shari Halpern

Time to Sleep
by Denise Fleming

Rosie's Walk
by Pat Hutchins

········ STORYTELLING ········
The Rabbit and the Elephant

WEEKS 3 AND 4
 **What the Sun Sees,
What the Moon Sees**
by Nancy Tafuri

Abuela
by Arthur Dorros

The Little House
by Virginia Lee Burton

WIGGLEWORKS PLUS: **City Sounds**

WEEKS 5 AND 6
 Hattie and the Fox
by Mem Fox

Madeline's Rescue
by Ludwig Bemelmans

Officer Buckle and Gloria
by Peggy Rathmann

 WIGGLEWORKS PLUS:
Music Is in the Air

PHONOLOGICAL AWARENESS PHONICS
M N O P Q R -an, -op

Alphabatics
by Suse MacDonald

- **Mentor:** Pat Mora,
  an author
- **Place:** Author's Studio

PHONOLOGICAL AWARENESS PHONICS
S T U V W X -at, -un, -ig

Amazon Alphabet
by Martin and Tanis Jordan

- **Mentor:** Steven Powell,
  a farmer
- **Place:** Gardening Center

PHONOLOGICAL AWARENESS PHONICS
Y Z -en, -ot, CVC words

ABCDrive!
by Naomi Howland

- **Mentor:** Tom Chapin,
  a singer
- **Place:** Performance Stage

SETTING UP THE PLACE

Why an Author's Studio?

"We writers are always looking, smelling, touching, listening, observing to see how we can use something in our writing."

Pat Mora

Create a Workplace Model

A small section of your classroom can become a private office where young writers can work quietly and explore creative ideas. Provide plenty of idea resources, as well as a variety of materials to inspire children.

View the Mentor Video

Talk with children about the ways people tell stories. Discuss how the books they read tell stories with words and pictures. Then tell them that they are going to watch a video about an author, Pat Mora. Show children *Listen to the Desert,* a book written by Pat Mora. Then view the mentor video together.

Idea List

Keep an ongoing list of children's interests and ideas to which both you and children can contribute. Children can refer to this list when looking for new writing ideas.

Author's Chair

Provide a large comfortable chair for the authors to sit in when talking to audiences about their books. A special chair with a pillow can be used to set the author's chair apart from others in the classroom.

Desk

Sometimes authors need privacy and quiet to create. You can section off the author's desk so that it provides young writers with a feeling of seclusion.

Quiet.
Writer
at Work

Reference Library

Reference materials can include picture dictionaries, labeled pictures, individual word boxes, information books, magazines, storybooks, and child-made books.

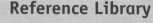

Message Board

Did you find my books?

ANN, I LIKE YOU!

Nature Guide

Birds

The Day

My Cat

Picture Dictionary

Short Stories

Story

Message Board

Set up a place for authors to leave notes to themselves and to one another. Messages can be written on sticky notes and attached to the board, or on scrap paper and taped.

Writing Supplies

Different kinds of materials inspire different kinds of writing. Paper can range in size, texture, and color. Writing implements can include regular and colored pencils, crayons, and markers. Envelopes (save those sent with junk mail) can be used with letters.

WEEKS 1 AND 2

Kindergarten Goals
for Weeks 1 and 2

Oral Language/ Vocabulary

- participating in rhymes, songs, conversations, and discussions
- participating in choral reading
- discussing sound words, body part words, and bedtime words
- exploring story vocabulary

Reading

- building alphabetic knowledge
- participating actively in shared reading
- engaging in emergent reading
- making predictions
- exploring concepts of print
- using pictures to gather information
- chiming in on patterned text
- identifying rhyme and repeated sounds
- reading high-frequency words

Writing

- writing sentences in sequence
- innovating on text pattern
- writing action words
- writing letters: *Mm, Nn*
- writing a chant
- making a sound word web
- creating an animal character bulletin board
- engaging in shared writing
- writing independently in Journals

Listening/Speaking/ Viewing

- listening responsively to stories and other texts read aloud
- identifying rhyming words
- listening to check predictions
- developing phonological awareness
- dramatizing stories
- retelling a story
- contributing to group discussions
- relating personal experiences to literature
- demonstrating visual literacy

Daily Phonics: *Mm* and *Nn*

- reciting classic poems, songs, and nursery rhymes
- naming and recognizing the letters
- recognizing initial sounds
- recognizing sound/letter relationships
- generating words that begin with letter sounds
- decoding words using beginning sounds /m/, /n/
- blending words with *-an*

Center Workshops and Project

- acquiring world knowledge through cross-curricular activities
- creating an "Animals Say Hello" big book

Big Book

Meet the Author
Pat Mora, a native of El Paso, Texas, received a poetry fellowship in 1994.

Meet the Illustrator
Francisco X. Mora was born in Mexico and now lives in Wisconsin.

- **With Sentence Strips**

Available as audiocassette

Big Book of Rhymes and Rhythms

For teaching phonological awareness, the alphabet, and concepts of print.

- **"One Misty Moisty Morning"**
- **"The Little Nut Tree"**

Available as audiocassette

Read Aloud

Meet the Author/ Illustrator
Steven Kellogg gets many of his book ideas from memories of his childhood relationships. He enjoys taking long walks in the woods while he is thinking about a new book.

Read Aloud

Meet the Author/ Illustrator
Linnea Riley used sponges to spread watercolor on paper. Then each detail was cut and assembled into an illustration. She has also illustrated *Outside, Inside* and *The Twelve Days of Christmas*.

ABC Book

Meet the Author/ Illustrator
Suse MacDonald was born and raised in Illinois. *Alphabatics* was named one of *School Library Journal*'s Best Books of the Year and was selected a Caldecott Honor Book by the ALA.

Side One

Side Two

SourceCard

- Pat Mora is telling a story.
- "Eensy, Weensy Spider"

High-Frequency Reader

My Read and Write Book

My Alphabet Book

ESL/ELD Teaching Guide

My Books

To take home to share.

Introducing the Mentor

Pat Mora now lives in Santa Fe, New Mexico, where she enjoys writing in an adobe house. She is Latina and uses English and Spanish words in her stories.

DAYS AT A GLANCE

WEEKS 1 AND 2

	Daily Phonics	Literature	Shared Writing	Workshops and Projects
DAY 1	Phonological Awareness: Oral Segmentation: Beginning Sounds Review /j/j, /k/k, /l/l	*Alphabatics* by Suse MacDonald ABC BOOK	Write Sentences in Sequence	Art: Collage *Aa* to *Zz* Dramatic Play: Animal Act
DAY 2	**Consonant /m/m** Phonological Awareness: Rhyme	*Listen to the Desert/ Oye al desierto* by Pat Mora illustrated by Francisco X. Mora BIG BOOK · LITTLE BOOK	Innovate on the Story Pattern	Art: In the Desert Science: What's That Sound?
DAY 3	**Consonant /m/m** Phonological Awareness: Alliteration Introduce Sound-Spelling	*Listen to the Desert/ Oye al desierto* by Pat Mora BIG BOOK · LITTLE BOOK **High Frequency Reader:** *We Can Go!*	Concepts of Print: Commas Write *Mm* Make a Class Book	Music & Movement: Listen to This! Science: Desert Dioramas
DAY 4	**Consonant /m/m** Phonological Awareness: Oral Blending Review Sound-Spelling	*A-Hunting We Will Go!* by Steven Kellogg READ ALOUD	Focus on Action Words	Music & Movement: Strike Up the Band! Dramatic Play: Play House
DAY 5	**Consonant /m/m** Phonological Awareness: Alliteration Maintain Sound-Spelling	**"One Misty Moisty Morning"** a rhyme *Alphabatics* **My Book:** *"Meow," Said the Kitten*	Concepts of Print: Word Boundaries High-Frequency Word: *go*	Listening: Monday, Monday Art: *Mm* Mobiles

	Daily Phonics	Literature	Shared Writing	Workshops and Projects
DAY 6	**Consonant /n/n** Phonological Awareness: Auditory Discrimination	*Let's Get the Rhythm* by Anna Miranda	Write a Chant	Art: Express Yourself Vest Science: Body Words Match
DAY 7	**Consonant /n/n** Phonological Awareness: Oddity Task: Beginning Sound Introduce Sound-Spelling	**SourceCard** Pat Mora Is Telling a Story. "Eensy, Weensy Spider" **High-Frequency Reader:** *We Can Go!*	Make a Sound Word Web Write *Nn*	Dramatic Play: Play Charades Games: Sounds and Stories
DAY 8	**Consonant /n/n** Phonological Awareness: Oral Blending Review Sound-Spelling Phonogram *-an*	*Mouse Mess* by Linnea Riley READ ALOUD	Animal Character Story Book	Cooking: Animal Crackers Art: Make a Mouse House
DAY 9	**Consonant /n/n** Phonological Awareness: Auditory Discrimination Maintain Sound-Spelling	"The Little Nut Tree" a nursery rhyme *Mouse Mess* **My Book:** *It's Playtime*	Concepts of Print: Word Boundaries	Science: *Nn* Nests Math: My Number Book
DAY 10	Oral Blending: Review Beginning Sounds: Review	**Review Books from Weeks 1 and 2**	Make a Compare and Contrast Chart	Project: "Animals Say Hello" Big Book

Share the ABC Book

CHILDREN WILL:

- orally segment words (beginning sounds)
- review consonants /j/j, /k/k, and /l/l
- read and respond to *Alphabatics*
- recognize *Mm* and *Nn*
- focus on letter shapes
- write sentences about pictures
- explore story vocabulary
- engage in Center Workshops

MATERIALS

- *Eating the Alphabet*
- *Alphabatics*

GUIDED READING

To conclude each day's reading session, meet with guided reading groups. You might use Scholastic's Guided Reading Library or other books in your library.

Warm-Up: Wordplay

Ⓐ PHONOLOGICAL AWARENESS

Sound Toss Have children sit in a circle. Toss a ball to a child.

- Have the child who catches the ball say his or her name. Repeat the name, emphasizing the beginning sound: *L-L-Luis*.
- Encourage the child to think of a word that has the same beginning sound: *l-l-lettuce*.
- Invite children to continue tossing the ball around the circle until everyone has had a turn.

Ⓑ PHONICS MAINTENANCE

Review Consonants /j/j, /k/k, /l/l Have children chant the alphabet in order as you page through *Eating the Alphabet*. Stop on the pages containing the letters *j, k,* and *l.* Ask children to say the sound that each letter stands for. Then invite them to name a food that begins with each sound (such as *jam, ketchup,* or *lettuce*).

Build Background

ORAL LANGUAGE: FAVORITE THINGS TO DRAW

Ask children to name their favorite things to draw. List their ideas on chart paper in a column called *We Draw*. Also list the art supplies that children mention in a column called *We Use*. Then read the words together and ask children:

▶ **Which words are very short? Which are very long?**

▶ **Do you see any of these words in the classroom?**

PREVIEW AND PREDICT

Display the cover of Suse MacDonald's *Alphabatics*. Read the title and author/illustrator's name, tracking the print.

▶ **What letter is in the box on the cover? Can you name the toy the letter turns into? Why do you think the author put them on the cover together?**

Read the ABC Book

ALPHABETIC KNOWLEDGE: *Mm* AND *Nn*

Open *Alphabatics* and show children the first page. Invite them to explain what they see. Point out that the "A" in the picture is slowly turning into an Ark. Help children notice that the word *Ark* begins with the letter *A*. While you read, encourage children to predict the letter and the object that will be highlighted on the following page.

Stop at the pages for *Mm* and *Nn*. Invite children to say the names of the letters and to notice the uppercase and lowercase forms. Have them name the objects on each page and note the /**m**/ and /**n**/ sounds.

Alphabatics

Respond to the Literature

TALK ABOUT IT

Share Personal Responses Engage children in a conversation about the ABC book, letting them ask questions and share reactions. Remind children to raise their hand during a discussion and not to interrupt others.

▶ **Which was your favorite picture? Can you tell how the letter turned into that picture?**

▶ **Are there things in the book that you had never heard of before? Which ones?**

▶ **What would you draw on a page that shows the letter *Mm*?**

THINK ABOUT IT

Focus on Letter Shapes Have children focus on letter shapes. Have them look at the ***Aa*** page in *Alphabatics*. Remind them that every letter has its own special shape. Tell children that the shape for *A* reminded the author/illustrator of something she liked to draw: an ark. Together describe the shape of *A*.

• Its sides are straight lines.

• The sides lean against each other.

• A straight line touches both sides in the middle.

Ask volunteers to choose pages in the book and to name the highlighted letter. Discuss the shape of the uppercase or lowercase form of each letter using the illustration.

ESL/ELD

▲ Encourage children to also go through the book and show things that are new to them. For the /m/ and /n/ sounds, go around the room and see if you can find objects whose names begin with these sounds. To practice the /m/ sound, ask: *What do we say when we eat something we like?* (Rub tummy and say *mmmm!*) **(MAKE CONNECTIONS)**

OBSERVATION

Do children understand the connection between the object and letter on each page?

GIFTED & TALENTED

✳ **After reading and discussing the letters in Suse MacDonald's *Alphabatics*, children may enjoy playing this drawing game. Form small groups and ask a child in each group to think of a letter. Have the child describe the shape of the letter to his or her teammates without naming the letter. Teammates can draw the shape and try to guess the mystery letter. (MULTISENSORY)**

Shared Writing

WRITE SENTENCES IN SEQUENCE

Ask children to tell what is happening in the illustration on the *Aa* page of the ABC book. Point to each box and have children tell what the letter is doing. Guide them to say a complete sentence. For example: *The "A" fell in the water*. Invite children to help you write the sentences on chart paper by providing the letters that stand for the sounds they know. Then ask:

▶ **What letter in a sentence should be capitalized?**

▶ **What punctuation should come at the end of a sentence?**

Read the sentences aloud. Then repeat the activity with other pages.

Repeated Reading

EXPLORE STORY VOCABULARY

Reread the ABC book with children. Help children understand unusual vocabulary words by examining the pictures.

▶ **What does an ark remind you of? Where would you use an ark?**

▶ **Has anyone ever heard a xylophone? How do you play it?**

▶ **Where have you seen a clown? What did the clown do?**

READ AND WRITE INDEPENDENTLY

Journal Encourage children to reread Suse MacDonald's *Alphabatics* on their own or in small groups. Children can write in their Journals about their favorite letter page.

⊘ Comprehension Check

ACT IT OUT

As you page through the book, have children act out what is happening in the illustrations. For example, children can pretend to be sailing on an ark, chasing a balloon, or juggling like a clown.

HOME/SCHOOL CONNECTION

Give children the Family Newsletter from My Read and Write Book to bring home. Read the Newsletter to children and talk about what is on it. Discuss what children will say to their parents about the Newsletter and what they will be doing in school.

CENTER WORKSHOPS

Art

MATERIALS

- Paper
- Catalogs and nature magazines
- Glue
- Scissors
- Crayons or markers

Collage Aa to Zz

Invite children to use pictures of objects and animals to create ABC collages. Have them look through magazines and catalogs to find pictures they like. After children have cut out the pictures, help them name and sort the objects by the beginning sounds. Have them paste the pictures for *Aa* on a piece of paper and label it. Then ask them to continue making collages for the other letters of the alphabet.

Observation: Notice how children sort the pictures they cut out.

Dramatic Play

MATERIALS

- Construction paper
- Scissors
- Markers or crayons
- Yarn
- Glue
- *Alphabatics*

Animal Act

Encourage children to look through Suse MacDonald's *Alphabatics* and choose a favorite animal. Have them look at details in the illustrations and use construction paper to create a mask that represents the animal they chose.

Then suggest that children use props from the Dramatic Play Center to act out scenarios from the book. Encourage them to tell something about their animals during the performance: *I am an elephant. My name begins with Ee. I do tricks at the circus.*

Observation: How do children use prior knowledge to interpret the illustrations from the book?

DAY 2 OBJECTIVES

CHILDREN WILL:

- recognize rhyming words
- recognize /m/
- explore concepts about the desert
- read and respond to *Listen to the Desert*
- focus on animal sound words
- write about outdoor sounds
- engage in Center Workshops

MATERIALS

- *Listen to the Desert*
- **My Read and Write Book,** pp. 5–6

The Big Book is available on audiocassette in the Literacy Place Listening Center.

The song is available on the **Sounds of Phonics** audiocassette.

Share the Big Book

DAILY PHONICS

Consonant /m/m

PHONOLOGICAL AWARENESS

Rhyme Read aloud the title of the song "Miss Mary Mack." Ask children what sound they hear at the beginning of the words *Miss, Mary,* and *Mack.*

- Invite children to repeat the words as you exaggerate the beginning sound. For example: *M-M-Miss.*
- Sing or play the song. Invite children to sing along.
- During later singings, have children clap when they hear words that rhyme with *Mack (black, back)*.

Miss Mary Mack

Miss Mary Mack, Mack, Mack
All dressed in black, black, black
With silver buttons, buttons, buttons,
All down her back, back, back.

Build Background

ORAL LANGUAGE: THE DESERT

Show a desert picture. Ask children what they can tell about the desert from the picture.

▶ **What do you think the weather is like in the desert?**

▶ **What kinds of plants and animals might live there?**

▶ **How does the desert compare to where we live?**

PREVIEW AND PREDICT

Show the cover of *Listen to the Desert*. Read the title in English pointing to each word. Explain that the next line, *Oye al desierto,* tells the title in Spanish. Point out that the author is Pat Mora, whom they met in the Meet the Mentor Video.

SET A PURPOSE

Show the pictures of the desert and ask children to predict what they would hear if they "listened to the desert."

Read the Big Book

LISTEN IN TWO LANGUAGES

Read aloud *Listen to the Desert.* Read the Spanish as well as the English so that children can hear and enjoy the sound of the two languages.

- If you are not fluent in Spanish but have Spanish-speaking children in class, invite them to help you with pronunciation or to read the Spanish text to the group.

The repetitive structure of the book is ideal for echo-reading—in English or in Spanish. You read one line and children can "read" the next line by repeating what they have just heard.

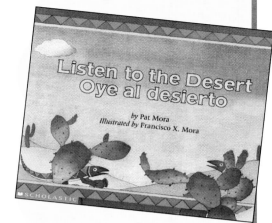

Listen to the Desert

Respond to the Literature

TALK ABOUT IT

Share Personal Responses Invite children to describe their favorite pages. Go back to check the predictions children made before you read the story.

▶ **Have you ever seen or heard of any of the animals in the book?**

▶ **Can you think of any other animals that might live in the desert?**

THINK ABOUT IT

Focus on Sound Words Talk with children about the sound that different animals make in the story.

- Name an animal and invite two volunteers to make its sound, one in English and the other in Spanish. List the animal and its sound on a chart.

- Invite children to imitate other animal sounds. Add the name of the animal and the corresponding sound to the chart.

Animal	English	Spanish
owl	whooo	uuu
coyote	ar-ar-aooo	ahúúú
fish	puh	plaf

MODIFY Instruction

ESL/ELD

▲ Have pairs of children draw two animals, cut them out, and mount them to be used as masks or puppets. The children can act out a "conversation" using the animal sound words on the chart in both languages. (ACT IT OUT)

MODIFY Instruction

GIFTED & TALENTED

✶ **Invite partners to write their own book about sounds that can be heard in a different environment. For example,** *Listen to the City; Jungle;* **or** *Circus.* **(WORK IN PAIRS)**

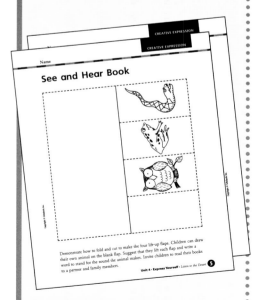

Name

See and Hear Book

Demonstrate how to fold and cut to make the four lift-up flaps. Children can draw their own animal on the blank flap. Suggest that they lift each flap and write a word to stand for the sound the animal makes. Invite children to read their books to a partner and family members.
Unit 4 • Express Yourself • *Listen to the Desert* ⑤

My Read and Write Book, pp. 5–6

Shared Writing

INNOVATE ON THE STORY PATTERN

Invite children to go outside on a listening walk. Remind them that they will need to be very quiet in order to hear the softest outdoor sounds. When you return, children can share their outdoor experiences in writing by completing the following sentence.

Listen to the _____.

LABEL CLASSROOM SOUNDS

Encourage children to identify different sounds they hear in the classroom. Help them write the word for each sound on a sticky note and attach it to the item. (Clock: *tick-tock;* Jackets being zipped: *zzzip;* Door: *slam*)

Repeated Reading

ADD SOUND EFFECTS

Let children have fun making the sound effects as you reread the book. For example, you read "Listen to the Desert," and the children can say "pon, pon, pon."

- Read the book in English, with children supplying the English sound effects.
- Read it again in Spanish, with children supplying the Spanish sound effects.
- The rhythm of the languages will help children know when it's time to produce the sounds, even when the reading is not in their first language.

READ AND WRITE INDEPENDENTLY

Journal Place copies of *Listen to the Desert* and the *Listen to the Desert* audiocassette in the Reading Center for children to enjoy on their own or in small groups. Children might enjoy writing in their Journals about other animals and the sounds that they make.

☑ Comprehension Check

ACT IT OUT

Read the story aloud once more. Invite children to echo the sounds again, but this time, invite them to add movements to the sounds. Encourage them to move their bodies in a way that captures the feeling of the animals or the weather conditions.

CENTER WORKSHOPS

In the Desert

Invite children to create a mural that shows a desert environment like the one in the story. Brown butcher paper will provide a background the color of sand on which children can paint cacti and the animals that appear in the story. The pictures in *Listen to the Desert* can serve as a reference for the children's work. Encourage children to consult other books about deserts and desert animals to get more ideas about what they can add to the mural. Label the mural by writing sentences.

Observation: How do children use *Listen to the Desert* and other books for reference while planning their mural?

MATERIALS

- **Brown butcher paper**
- **Paints and brushes**
- ***Listen to the Desert/Oye al desierto***

What's That Sound?

Fill pairs of margarine containers with identical objects. Put the containers in the Science Center. Invite children to shake the tubs and listen to the sounds. When children think they've matched two tubs with the same items, they can check to see if they are right.

For variety, have a child put something in one of the containers without letting others see. Challenge the rest of the class to shake the tub and guess what's inside. When everyone has made a guess, open the container to reveal what's in it.

Observation: Notice how children describe different sounds as they play the games.

MATERIALS

- **Plastic margarine containers**
- **Small natural objects that will fit in the containers, such as pebbles, sand, seeds, dried beans, bark, acorns, nuts, twigs, and pine cones**

DAY 3 OBJECTIVES

CHILDREN WILL:

- listen for alliteration
- recognize /m/m and write *Mm*
- reread *Listen to the Desert*
- participate in choral reading
- recognize commas
- identify high-frequency word: *go*
- read the High-Frequency Reader: *We Can Go!*
- engage in Center Workshops

MATERIALS

- *Listen to the Desert*
- Sentence Strips for *Listen to the Desert*
- High-Frequency Reader: *We Can Go!*
- My Alphabet Book, p. 15
- My Read and Write Book, p. 7

The Big Book is available on audiocassette in the Literacy Place Listening Center.

My Alphabet Book, p. 15

Revisit the Big Book

and Read the High-Frequency Reader

Consonant /m/m

Ⓐ PHONOLOGICAL AWARENESS

Alliteration Write the following alliterative sentence on the chalkboard:

Mary Moose munches mulberry muffins on Monday.

Read aloud the sentence, and have children repeat it. Then ask them to count how many times they hear **/m/**.

Ⓑ CONNECT SOUND-SPELLING

Introduce Consonant /m/m Page through *Alphabatics* until you get to the *Mm* page. Point out to children that the letter *m* stands for **/m/** as in **mustache.**

- Ask children to say the sound with you.
- Point to the mustache on the page and ask children to exaggerate **/m/** at the beginning of the word.

Letter Formation

WRITE THE LETTER

Write *Mm* on the chalkboard. Point out the capital and small forms of the letter. Model how to write the letter using the rhymes provided below.

- Have children write both forms of the letter. Ask them to make the letter's sound as they practice writing.
- Observe chidren's pencil grip, paper position, and beginning stroke as they write.

M	m
Down, *(Pull down straight.)* Down, up, down. *(Slant down right, slant up right, pull down straight.)* Make two mountains for our town.	Down and up. *(Pull down straight, retrace up.)* Over and down, over and down. *(Pull over and down, over and down.)* To make two mini-mounds for our town.

Reread the Big Book

OPTIONS

Choral Reading Invite children to use the book's pattern, the picture clues, and their knowledge of animal sounds to perform a choral reading. Invite one group of children to read the first line and a second group to read the second line. Spanish-speaking children or a teacher can read the Spanish portion.

Decoding Strategies Point out to children that they can use the letters and sounds they have learned to figure out how to pronounce words.

Stop before the words *dove, fish,* and *mice.* Point to the first letter and have children say the sound. Help them use the letter-sound relationship along with the picture clue and story pattern to read the words.

READ AND WRITE INDEPENDENTLY

Journal Place copies of *Listen to the Desert* in the Reading Center for children to read alone or in small groups. Children can write in their Journals about sounds they hear in their own environment.

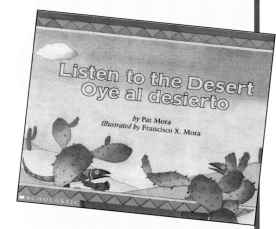

Listen to the Desert

Concepts of Print

PUNCTUATION: COMMAS

Display the Sentence Strips. Read the first strip, pausing at each comma. Point out the punctuation mark to children and explain that it is called a *comma.* Explain that a comma tells you to pause. Then invite volunteers to find the commas in the other sentences. Read the sentences together, pausing at each comma.

Listen to the desert, pon, pon, pon.

Listen to the owl hoot, whoo, whoo, whoo.

Listen to the toad hop, plop, plop, plop.

Listen to the snake hiss, tst-tst-tst, tst-tst-tst.

Listen to the dove say coo, coo, coo.

MODIFY Instruction

EXTRA HELP

◼ Children may enjoy recording themselves making sounds of the desert. Encourage them to name an animal and then imitate the sound it makes, for example: "owl, whoo, whoo, whoo." When children have finished recording desert sounds, play back the audiocassette and invite them to chime in. **(USE AUDIO)**

Written by Ellen Geist
Illustrated by Ken Bowser

SCHOLASTIC

We Can Go!

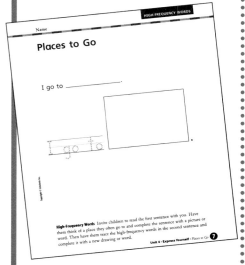

My Read and Write Book, p. 7

Read High-Frequency Reader

INTRODUCE THE BOOK

Display the book *We Can Go!* Read the title and the author's name. Explain that it tells about places that the children on the cover can go, if only in their imaginations.

▶ **Where are your favorite places to go? Where do you think the children on the book cover will want to go?**

HIGH-FREQUENCY WORD: go

On the board, write the sentence stem *We can go to the _____.* Underline the word *go.* Then write the word *go* on a note card. Read it aloud.

• Display the card and have children read the word.

• Help children spell it aloud, clapping on each letter.

• Ask children to write it in the air as they state aloud each letter.

Review the other high-frequency words: *We, can,* and *to.* Help volunteers find them on the Word Wall and read them aloud. Invite children to complete the sentence stem by naming places they go. Write each new sentence on the board. Have volunteers circle the word *go.*

Add the card for *go* to the Word Wall.

SHARE THE HIGH-FREQUENCY READER

Read the story aloud, tracking the print. Invite children to point to the high-frequency words *We, can, go, to,* and *the.*

• After each sentence, ask: *Do you want to go to this place too?* Encourage children to name similar places that they have visited or have imagined visiting.

• This story also reviews consonants /d/d, /j/j, and /l/l and includes words with /m/m and /n/n. Help children use their knowledge of these sound-spellings to decode words.

SHARED WRITING

Invite children to make a class book called *We Can Go!*

• Ask each child to think of a place they like to go. Help children write and complete the sentence stem *We can go to the _____.* Have them illustrate their sentences. Bind the pages into a book and share it with the class.

CENTER WORKSHOPS

Music & Movement

MATERIALS

- **Rhythm band instruments**
- **Tape recorder**

Listen to This!

Invite children to explore the concept of imitating sound with language. One child can use a rhythm band instrument to make a sound. The child's partner can try to imitate that sound with his or her voice. Children can record the two sounds and play back the tape to see if they sound the same.

You might prepare in advance a tape of sounds made with instruments. Children can listen to the tape, try to figure out what instrument made each sound, and reproduce the sound with their voice.

Observation: How do children experiment with different ways of using their voices?

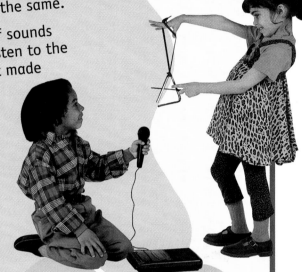

Science

MATERIALS

- **Shoeboxes**
- **Paints and brushes**
- **Sand**
- **Pebbles**
- **Glue**
- **Clay**
- **Construction paper**
- **Crayons**

Desert Dioramas

Invite children to create shoebox dioramas of the desert. Have them paint the inside of the boxes to make the sky and background for their desert scenes. They can glue pebbles and sand to the box bottoms for textured ground. Show children how to mold clay into plants and animals. Glue these into place.

Encourage children to share their completed dioramas with one another. Set up a museum area in the classroom to display them. Children may also wish to make labels or signs for their dioramas.

Observation: What plants and animals do children choose to make for their dioramas?

DAY 4 OBJECTIVES

CHILDREN WILL:

- orally blend word parts
- review consonant /m/m
- talk about bedtime
- read and respond to *A-Hunting We Will Go!*
- discuss genre: fantasy
- write action words
- listen for rhyme and repetition
- engage in Center Workshops

MATERIALS

- *A-Hunting We Will Go!*

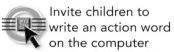

TECHNOLOGY

Invite children to write an action word on the computer using the **WiggleWorks Plus** Write area. Then have them create their own make-believe animal using the paint tools and show their creature doing that action.

For more computer activities, see the Technology Teaching Plan.

Share the Read Aloud

DAILY PHONICS

Consonant /m/m

(A) PHONOLOGICAL AWARENESS

Oral Blending State aloud the following word parts and ask children to blend them. Provide corrective feedback and modeling when necessary.

/m/ . . . ake	/m/ . . . op	/m/ . . . ess
/m/ . . . onkey	/m/ . . . ix	/m/ . . . ail

(B) CONNECT SOUND-SPELLING

Mouse-Hole Words Draw an outline of a mouse hole on chart paper. Write the word *mouse* and circle the letter *m.* Remind children that the letter *m* stands for **/m/.** Invite children to suggest words that begin with **/m/** to put in the mouse hole. Write each word and have volunteers circle the letter *m.*

Build Background

ORAL LANGUAGE: WHAT WE DO AT BEDTIME

Ask children to think about getting ready for bed.

▶ **What do your favorite pajamas look like?**

▶ **What is your favorite bedtime story or song?**

Then tell children that they will be reading a book about children getting ready for bed.

PREVIEW AND PREDICT

Read aloud the title, *A-Hunting We Will Go!* and the author/illustrator's name. Show children the music on the inside front cover. Hum the tune or sing the song as you point to the notes.

▶ **Do you know this song? Do you know the words?**

▶ **Do you think the children in the book will sing it?**

SET A PURPOSE

As children read, encourage them to predict what the characters will do next as they get ready for bed.

Share the Read Aloud

LISTEN FOR PLEASURE

Read the story to the tune of the song, "A-Hunting We Will Go!" Track the print, pointing out where the words are in speech balloons.

- When you reach the turning point in the story, guide children to understand that the characters are finally getting ready for bed.

A-Hunting We Will Go!

Respond to the Literature

TALK ABOUT IT

Share Personal Responses Encourage children to share their sense of wonderment at the improbable events in the story.

▶ **Would you like to go on an adventure like this?**

▶ **What was your favorite part of the story?**

▶ **Would you like to read this book at bedtime?**

SING A SONG

Point out again, the music for the song, "A-Hunting We Will Go!" on the inside cover. Children might enjoy singing the song as you flip through the pages.

THINK ABOUT IT

Recognize Fantasy Talk about how children can tell if this story is pretend or real. Page through the illustrations as you ask questions such as:

▶ **How would you describe this giraffe? Do real giraffes get tickled?**

▶ **Do bathtubs float? Is this like a real bathroom?**

▶ **How are the animals in this story different from the animals in *Listen to the Desert?***

Make sure children understand that the girl and boy are real, but that they are playing make-believe as they get ready for bed.

MODIFY Instruction

GIFTED & TALENTED

☀ Invite children to imagine what it might be like to eat breakfast with the animal friends in the story. Would the characters eat people food or animal food? Would the animals talk like people? Encourage children to act out the scenario for the class. **(ACT IT OUT)**

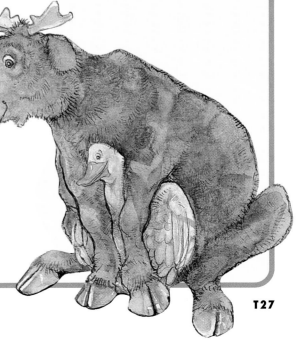

MODIFY Instruction

ESL/ELD

▲ Invite English language learners to invent movements for each verse or to act out the action words suggested by their classmates. Then switch roles and have English language learners give the action commands. (PANTOMIME)

PROFESSIONAL DEVELOPMENT

GAY SU PINNELL

Developing a Love for Reading

An important goal of early reading instruction is developing in students a love for reading. This can be developed by (1) showing your love of reading through sharing books of interest, (2) allowing students opportunities to self-select books, such as during daily independent reading time, and (3) providing children with early reading successes through the use of leveled materials they can read comfortably.

Shared Writing

FOCUS ON ACTION WORDS

Remind children of some of the things the characters do in the story: sing, laugh, hop, row. Together go through the book and look for other action words. Write these words on a chart.

- Invite children to create a new page for the story by picking an action word and drawing themselves doing the action in a silly situation.

- Help children label their drawings with the sentence "A-_____ , I will go!" Point out that children should add *ing* to the end of the action word they choose to complete the sentence. Tell them to add an exclamation point to their sentences.

Repeated Reading

CHIME IN ON RHYME AND REPETITION

Invite children to listen for a pattern as you reread the story.

- When they become acquainted with the refrain, encourage them to chime in on "A-hunting we will go!"

- Children might also like to clap their hands or jingle bells to the rhythm of the words.

You may want to read the book again to focus on the rhyming patterns. Have children identify words that rhyme on each page. Invite them to notice that the verses end with a word that rhymes with *go*.

READ AND WRITE INDEPENDENTLY

Journal Place *A-Hunting We Will Go!* in the Reading Center so children can read it independently. Invite children to draw pictures showing the story characters doing other unlikely things.

Encourage children to create stories in their Journals to go along with their pictures.

🎯 Comprehension Check

RETELL THE STORY

Invite volunteers to retell the story as you show the pictures. Remind them to speak clearly. On each page, ask children to point out something that is make-believe.

CENTER WORKSHOPS

Music & Movement

MATERIALS

- Pie tins
- Dried seeds/beans
- Margarine tubs
- Sand or rice
- Jelly jars, pan lids
- Thick rubber bands
- Small boxes

Strike Up the Band!

Invite children to work independently or in small groups to create musical instruments from recycled materials. Guide them as they explore the materials and the sounds each makes. Show them how to pluck a rubber band, rattle beans, and tap a jar filled with water.

Once the musical instruments are completed, set aside time for children to strike up the band. Children may wish to accompany a song on a tape. Or, they might wish to parade through the school playing their instruments and singing a favorite song.

Observation: Notice how children create different sounds as they experiment with the materials.

Dramatic Play

MATERIALS

- Dress-up clothes
- Toy bathroom props such a toothbrush, toothpaste, soap, and towel
- Small pillow and blanket

Play House

Encourage children to share their bedtime routines with one another by playing house in the Housekeeping Center. Have them take turns putting a "sister" or "brother" to bed, explaining the order in which to do things— for example, put on fuzzy slippers *before* reading a bedtime story.

- Alternatively, some children may wish to have a sleep-over and share with several classmates how they get ready for bed.

Observation: Notice if children adapt to each role. Do they feel comfortable giving instructions? Are they willing to follow instructions?

DAY 5 OBJECTIVES

CHILDREN WILL:

- orally segment words (beginning sounds)
- read a rhyme
- review /m/m
- frame words in a sentence
- review high-frequency words
- read My Book: *"Meow," Said the Kitten*
- engage in Center Workshops

MATERIALS

- *Big Book of Rhymes and Rhythms*, p. 18
- *My Read and Write Book*, p. 8
- *My Book: "Meow," Said the Kitten*
- *Sentence Strips for "One Misty Moisty Morning"*
- *ABC Card: Mm*
- *Alphabatics*

For additional practice, see *Scholastic Phonics K*, pp. 71–74. See also Sound and Letter Book: *Where Is the Muffin?*

My Read and Write Book, p. 8

Sounds and Letters

and Read My Book

Consonant /m/m

A PHONOLOGICAL AWARENESS

Alliteration Read aloud "One Misty Moisty Morning" from the *Big Book of Rhymes and Rhythms*. Ask children what sound they hear at the beginning of *Misty, Moisty,* and *Morning*. Invite children to repeat the words, isolating the **/m/** sound. Then have them name other words that begin with **/m/**.

B CONCEPTS OF PRINT

Place the *Big Book of Rhymes and Rhythms*, the Sentence Strips for "One Misty Moisty Morning," and a pocket chart in the Reading Center. Read the rhyme, asking children to move their arms in time with the rhythm.

- Reread the rhyme, one line at a time. Ask volunteers to place the corresponding Sentence Strip in a pocket chart.
- Invite volunteers to frame each word with their fingers. Review that there are spaces before and after words.
- Then have children point to words that begin with *Mm*.

Mm

One Misty Moisty Morning

One misty moisty morning,
When cloudy was the weather,
I chanced to meet an old man,
Clothed all in leather.
He began to compliment,
And I began to grin,
"How do you do?
And how do you do?
And how do you do again?"

Big Book of Rhymes and Rhythms, p. 18

One misty moisty morning,

When cloudy was the weather,

I chanced to meet an old man,

Clothed all in leather.

MODIFY
Instruction

ESL/ELD

▲ Have a fluent classmate team up with an English language learner to search for pictures in magazines or catalogs whose names begin with *m*. Together they can create an *m* collage. **(MULTISENSORY TECHNIQUES)**

Ⓒ **CONNECT SOUND-SPELLING**

Alphabetic Principle Point to the *Mm* ABC Card and have children name the letter and picture. Remind children that the letter *m* stands for /m/. Page through *Alphabatics* as children chant the letters of the alphabet. Briefly review the sound that each letter stands for, stopping on the letter *Mm*.

ABC Book Explain to children that they are going to make a new page for their own ABC book. Have children suggest animals, objects, and people whose names begin with /m/. When the list is complete, invite children to work together to create the *Mm* page for their ABC Books.

Make a Mitten Line Tell children to draw and cut out a mitten shape from a piece of drawing paper. Have them draw or cut and paste on the mitten a picture of an object whose name begins with /m/. Help children write the object's name under its picture. Hang children's mittens on a string to make a mitten line.

Ⓓ **VOCABULARY: HIGH-FREQUENCY WORDS**

Write the incomplete sentence *Can you go to the _____ ?* on the chalkboard. Then do the following:

• Review each high-frequency word in the sentence. If necessary, review the read-spell-write routine for each word.

• Place the word *park* in the blank space. Invite a volunteer to read the new sentence.

• Invite children to suggest new place names to complete the sentence.

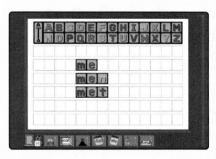

TECHNOLOGY

The **WiggleWorks Plus** Magnet Board activity pictured above provides additional practice with words that begin with *Mm*. Ask children to write the word *me.* Invite them to copy it three times and to add *n* and *t* to form new words.

The rhyme in the *Big Book of Rhymes and Rhythms* is available on the **Sounds of Phonics** audiocassette.

"Meow," Said the Kitten

MODIFY
Instruction

ESL/ELD

▲ After the class makes the sound of each animal in the story, ask English language learners to make the sound in their native language. Once you have gone through all the animals in the story, point to an animal and ask a volunteer to say the animal's name. Make sure children know that a *kitten* is a *baby cat.* **(MAKE CONNECTIONS)**

Read My Book

INTRODUCE THE BOOK

Let children know that they are going to get their own book that they can read on their own and take home.

▶ **What are some of the ways animals talk to one another?**

▶ **What sound does your favorite animal make?**

PREVIEW AND PREDICT

Pass out copies of *"Meow," Said the Kitten*. Read the title and the author's and illustrator's names. Ask children about the illustration on the cover.

▶ **What do you think these animals are doing? What do you think this book might be about?**

READ TOGETHER

Read the My Book with children, tracking the print as you read. Guide children to read along in their copies, and to make the sound that each animal makes.

PHONICS

Ask children to say the word *Meow* aloud.

▶ **What letter stands for the sound you hear at the beginning of the word?**

Help children use the sound-spelling patterns they have learned to read the animal names.

READ AND WRITE INDEPENDENTLY

Journal Encourage children to read *"Meow," Said the Kitten* on their own or in small groups. Provide crayons and invite children to color the illustrations.

HOME/SCHOOL CONNECTION

Children can take home their My Books to share with family members and friends. Suggest that children make a book of greetings they use with family members.

CENTER WORKSHOPS

Listening

MATERIALS

- **Tape recorder**
- **Oaktag strip with the following sentence:**
  On Monday morning, _____ likes to _____.

Monday, Monday

Invite children to work in groups to make a Monday morning tape. Display the Monday morning oaktag strip and have children read it aloud with you. Ask children to think of names and activities to complete the sentence. Encourage them to use as many words as possible that begin with the letter *Mm.* For example: *On Monday morning, Michael likes to climb a mountain.*

- Have each child record his or her sentence during the week.
- On Monday morning, invite children to listen to their recordings during their free time.

Observation: Notice if children can hear when their suggestions don't begin with /m/. Can they correct themselves?

Art

MATERIALS

- **Paper**
- **Magazines and catalogs**
- **Markers**
- **Paste or glue**
- **String**
- **Dowel rods or tree branches**
- **Tape**

Mm Mobiles

Place a variety of materials in the Art Center and invite children to make *Mm* Mobiles. Ask children to find pictures of items whose names begin with *Mm.* Have them paste the pictures on heavy paper, cut them into shapes, and tape them to string. Hang the pictures from dowel rods or tree branches. Display the mobiles in a prominent place.

Observation: Listen to the children talk about their *Mm* Mobiles. See if their conversation reflects an understanding of sound/letter relationships.

CHILDREN WILL:

- recognize /n/
- name parts of the body
- read and respond to *Let's Get the Rhythm*
- recognize story pattern and rhythm
- explore sounds and movements
- write a chant
- participate in a choral reading
- engage in Center Workshops

MATERIALS

- *Let's Get the Rhythm*
- My Read and Write Book, pp. 9–10

GUIDED READING

To conclude each day's reading session, meet with guided reading groups. You might use Scholastic's Guided Reading Library or other books in your library.

TECHNOLOGY

 Children can open the story in **WiggleWorks Plus** and choose the Read Aloud option. Encourage them to echo the lines as they are read.

 The song is available on the **Sounds of Phonics** audiocassette.

Share the WiggleWorks Book

DAILY PHONICS

Consonant /n/n

PHONOLOGICAL AWARENESS

Song Sing "The Noble Duke of York" to the tune of "A-Hunting We Will Go," emphasizing the /n/ in the word *Noble*. Then play or sing the song again, and have children emphasize the beginning /n/ in *noble*. Have children whose names begin with /n/ stand and say their names.

The Noble Duke of York

Oh, the noble Duke of York,
He had ten thousand men;
He marched them up to the top of the hill
And marched them down again.

Build Background

ORAL LANGUAGE: PARTS OF THE BODY

Hold up an arm and ask: *What is this called?* Point to your leg and have children name it. Continue pointing to, and inviting children to identify, your hand, foot, knee, and so on. Write each new word in a word web on the board. Invite children to illustrate the words.

When the web is done, teach children how to clap their hands rhythmically. Continue, teaching children to snap their fingers, stamp their feet, and slap their knees rhythmically.

PREVIEW AND PREDICT

Display the book, *Let's Get the Rhythm,* and read the title. Guide children to predict what the story will be about.

▶ **Who is on the cover? What are they doing? How do you think they feel?**

▶ **Why might the story be called *Let's Get the Rhythm*?**

Read the WiggleWorks Book

FOCUS ON RHYTHM

Turn to the illustration on page 3. Explain that the children in the picture are thinking of a game to play. Then begin reading. Once children figure out the pattern and rhythm of the story, encourage them to chime in as you read aloud.

Respond to the Literature

TALK ABOUT IT

Share Personal Responses Encourage children to have a conversation about the story.

▶ **Did you like joining in on the chant?**

▶ **Is this chant hard to learn? Why or why not?**

▶ **Would you like to play this game with the children?**

▶ **What game would you teach the children to play?**

THINK ABOUT IT

Explore Sounds and Movement Talk with children about how the story characters express themselves through sounds and movements.

• Ask how they think the characters feel as they act out different parts of the chant.

• Using illustrations, guide children to see how the characters perform similar actions in individual ways.

• Ask small groups of children to clap and snap in their own way as you chant the appropriate lines from the story.

Let's Get the Rhythm

MODIFY Instruction

ESL/ELD

▲ Before reading the story, teach English language learners the parts of the body mentioned in the chant. Cut out a photograph of a person and label the following: hands, feet, hips, knees, and head. Then read each label. Have children echo the name and point to that part of their body. If you wish, refer to the diagram as you read the story aloud. **(USE VISUALS)**

TECHNOLOGY

Invite children to get into the rhythm by recording the chant with the **WiggleWorks Plus** Record and Playback tools. As they listen to their recording, they can play the game themselves! Also consider making an exercise video with the class. Clapping your hands, stamping your feet, and shaking your head are all beneficial forms of exercise.

TECHNOLOGY

Tell children that *thunk* stands for the sound made by a book dropping on the floor. Using the **WiggleWorks Plus** Magnet Board, let children create words that stand for the sounds made by the activities in *Let's Get the Rhythm*. Each time they write a word, they should click the word to hear it.

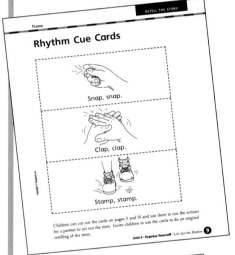

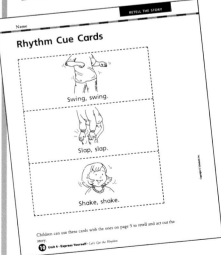

My Read and Write Book, pp. 9–10

WRITE A CHANT

Shared Writing

After reviewing the action words used in the story, encourage children to think of other words that could be used to play the game *Let's Get the Rhythm*. (Possibilities include: *tap, click, kick,* and *flap.*) Write the chant pattern on chart paper:

Let's get the rhythm of the game.

_____ , _____ .

Now you've got the rhythm of the game.

_____ , _____ .

Then invite children to write action words in the blanks to create additional verses for the chant.

CHORAL READING

Repeated Reading

Have children form two groups. Tell the groups to stand on opposite sides of the room. Read aloud the first page of the story. Then have one group read the pages that begin with *Let's get the rhythm . . .* , while the other group reads the pages that begin with *Now you've got the rhythm. . . .* Have both groups read the last line of the story together. Encourage children to speak clearly and loudly.

READ AND WRITE INDEPENDENTLY

Journal Place *Let's Get the Rhythm* in the Reading Center so children can read it in groups of six. Have children read the opening and closing pages together, and each child in the group read one verse of the chant. Encourage children to write and draw in their Journals about group games they enjoy playing.

☑ Comprehension Check

ACT IT OUT

Gather in a large open area and invite children to move to the rhythm of the chant and to perform the actions as you or a child reads it aloud.

CENTER WORKSHOPS

Art

Express Yourself Vest

Invite children to express themselves by decorating paper vests and wearing them as they act out *Let's Get the Rhythm*.

- Ask children to think about how the chant makes them feel. Then have them decorate their vests to reflect these feelings.
- Encourage children to wear their vests as they teach the chant to family members or friends.

Observation: Note the feelings that children express in their artwork.

MATERIALS

- **Vests cut from large grocery bags**
- **Construction paper**
- **Paste, scissors**
- **Markers, crayons**
- **Ribbon**
- **Buttons and other decorative materials**

Science

Body Words Match

Guide children in creating a matching game using words from the story that name parts of the body: *hands, feet, hips, knees,* and *head.*

- Have children write each word on a card.
- Then have them draw or cut out a picture of each part of the body and put it on another card.

Invite children to match the word for each body part to its corresponding picture.

If children need help remembering the meaning of a word, suggest that they use picture clues in *Let's Get the Rhythm*.

Observation: Notice how children match the words and pictures.

MATERIALS

- **Ten index cards**
- **Markers or crayons**
- **Glue**
- **Old magazines**

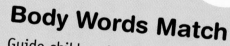

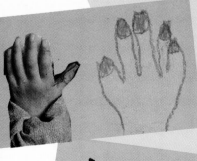

DAY 7 OBJECTIVES

CHILDREN WILL:

- recognize /n/
- Identify /n/n and write *Nn*
- sing a song
- create a place-and-sound word web
- review the high-frequency words
- revisit *We Can Go!*
- explore long and short words
- engage in Center Workshops

MATERIALS

- Picture Cards, R33–R34
- *Alphabatics*
- *Creative Expression*, SourceCard 1
- *Listen to the Desert/Oye al desierto*
- High-Frequency Reader: *We Can Go!*
- My Alphabet Book, p. 16

TECHNOLOGY

 Encourage children to use the drawing and writing tools in the **WiggleWorks Plus** Write area to complete the activities in this session.

My Alphabet Book, p. 16

Read the SourceCard

 **DAILY PHONICS**  *and Read the High-Frequency Reader*

Consonant /n/n

(A) PHONOLOGICAL AWARENESS

Oddity Task: Beginning Sounds Show the following sets of picture cards. Have children name them. Ask: *Which two words begin with the same sound? What is that sound?*

- bat, nest, nose
- cup, nest, nut
- nose, nut, fish
- nut, dog, nose

(B) CONNECT SOUND-SPELLING

Introduce Consonant /n/n Page through *Alphabatics* singing the alphabet until you get to the *Nn* page. Read the word *nest,* isolating the beginning sound: /n/. Point out the initial consonant *n* and explain that it stands for the sound at the beginning of *nest.*

- Ask children to say the sound **/n/** with you.
- Invite children to think of other words that begin with **/n/.** Write them on the board. Have volunteers circle the letter *n.*

Letter Formation

WRITE THE LETTER

Write *Nn* on the chalkboard. Point out the uppercase and lowercase forms of the letter.

- Have children write both forms of the letter in the air with their fingers. Ask children to make the letter's sound as they practice writing. Use the rhymes below as you demonstrate how the letters are formed.

N	n
Here's my needle, watch it go. Down, up, *(Pull down straight. Lift up.)* Down, up, *(Slant down to right. Pull straight up.)* As I sew.	Dad pulls his necktie down so straight. *(Pull down straight.)* Up, over, down again. . . it looks great! *(Retrace up, over, and down.)*

Share the SourceCard

SIDE ONE

Meet an Author Show children the cover of the book *Listen to the Desert* and point out the author's name, Pat Mora. Remind children that they viewed a video about Pat Mora.

Explain to children that Pat Mora enjoys telling her stories as well as writing them down. Then display side one of the SourceCard and read aloud the sentence.

▶ **What do you think the story she is telling might be about?**

▶ **Do you think Pat Mora is making sounds during the storytelling?**

▶ **What parts of her body is she using to tell the story?**

▶ **What are the children doing?**

SIDE TWO

Be a Storyteller Invite children who know this familiar song to teach it to the whole class, using the gestures that go with the words. Then have a small group of children give a storytelling performance by humming the tune of the song and making the gestures.

Side One
Pat Mora is telling a story.

Side Two

Eensy, Weensy Spider

The eensy, weensy spider
Went up the water spout.
Down came the rain
And washed the spider out.

Out came
the sun
and dried
up all the rain.

The eensy, weensy spider
Went up the spout again.

Shared Writing

MAKE A SOUND WORD WEB

Ask the class to imagine being in different places and to name the sounds they would hear in each place. Together make a word web of the places and sounds. Some ideas might include: hearing whistles and chugging at a train station; hearing cheeps and roars at a zoo. Invite children to write the letters they know. After children have completed the web, read the sound words together.

MODIFY Instruction

ESL/ELD

▲ Model the hand motions of the Eensy, Weensy Spider as you read the words. Have children copy your actions. Encourage those who are able to chant the words as well. Point out that *eensy, weensy* means very small. **(MODEL)**

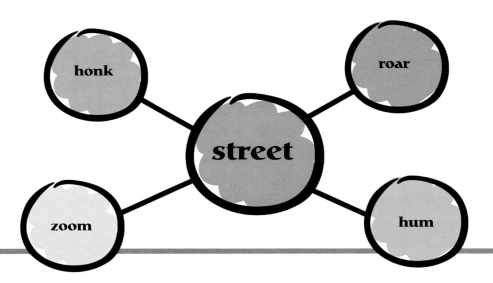
honk · street · roar · zoom · hum

We Can Go!

Revisit High-Frequency Reader

REREAD THE BOOK

Invite children to join you as you read *We Can Go!* again. On the first page have children read the words in the sentence that they have already learned *(We, can, go, to, the)*. Review these words.

DECODING STRATEGIES

As you go through the book, point to each word, the picture clue, the initial letter, and any other sound-spellings children have learned. Model blending words as needed. For example, have children use their knowledge of /l/ to help decode the word *library*.

Think Aloud *At the beginning of the word, I see the letter l. I know that l stands for /l/. In the picture, I see a library. The word* library *begins with /l/. This word is* library. *That makes sense in this sentence.*

CONCEPTS OF PRINT: LONG AND SHORT WORDS

Cut apart the words for one sentence strip. Discuss the fact that most of the words in the sentence are short. Invite children to find the one word that is long—*library*. Repeat with other sentence strips.

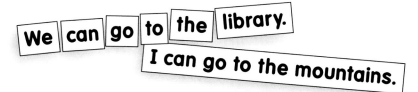

ORAL LANGUAGE: BOOKS

Invite children to talk about different kinds of books and what we can learn from reading them.

READ FOR FLUENCY

Give each child their own copy of *We Can Go!* Have children read the first page together to find out where the children can go together. Then have them read the remaining pages to find out where each individual child can go.

READ AND WRITE INDEPENDENTLY

Journal Place copies of *We Can Go!* in the Reading Center for children to read independently. Children can draw or write about a place they like to go.

HOME/SCHOOL CONNECTION

Children can take home their copies of *We Can Go!* to share with family members. They can create a new page about a place that would be exciting to visit.

CENTER WORKSHOPS

Dramatic Play

Play Charades

Invite children to imitate the sound of an animal or a machine.

- First have children cut out from magazines pictures of things that make sounds. Place the pictures in a box.
- Ask children to take turns picking a picture from the box and pantomiming the way the animal or machine moves.
- The actor can give an extra clue by imitating the way the animal or machine sounds.

If you wish, you can extend the activity by letting children sort the pictures into categories.

Observation: How do children decide which pictures to cut out for the box?

MATERIALS

- **Magazines**
- **Scissors**
- **Box**

Games

Sounds and Stories

Cut construction paper into four squares. In each square, ask children to draw a picture of an animal or object that makes a sound.

- Ask four children to choose a card.
- Have a child start a story about their picture and make the object's sound.
- Then have the others add a sentence to the story after looking at their own pictures.

If an instant camera is available, take the class for a walk, letting volunteers take pictures of things that make sounds.

Observation: How do children incorporate their animal or object and its sound into the group story?

MATERIALS

- **Construction paper**
- **Scissors**
- **Crayons**
- **Camera (optional)**

Share the Read Aloud

CHILDREN WILL:

- orally blend words with /n/ (beginning and ending)
- blend words with phonogram *-an*
- read and respond to *Mouse Mess*
- focus on sound words
- talk about plot
- write about animal characters
- engage in Center Workshops

MATERIALS

- *Mouse Mess*

TECHNOLOGY

 Children might enjoy viewing the video *Mouse Around*, available from Weston Woods.

DAILY PHONICS

Consonant /n/n

Ⓐ PHONOLOGICAL AWARENESS

Oral Blending Say aloud the following word parts, and ask children to blend them. Provide corrective feedback.

/n/...ose   /n/...ine   /n/...ap
pe.../n/   wi.../n/   ru.../n/

Ⓑ CONNECT SOUND-SPELLING

Introduce the Phonogram *-an* Write the phonogram *-an* on the chalkboard. Review with children that *n* stands for **/n/** as in *nest*. Say the sounds that *-an* stands for. Add the letter *c* to the beginning of *-an* and blend the sounds to form the word *can*. Remind children that *c* stands for **/k/**.

Think Aloud *I can put the letters* c *and* an *together to make the word* can. *Let's say the word slowly as I move my fingers under the letters. Listen to how I string together the sounds to make the word.* cccaaannn, ccaann, can.

Ⓒ BLEND

List the following words and sentences on the chalkboard. Have children read each word or sentence chorally. Model blending where necessary.

- **can**   • **fan**   • **man**   • **I like the fan.**

Build Background

ORAL LANGUAGE: ANIMAL CHARACTERS

Invite children to discuss favorite animal characters.

▶ **What is your favorite animal story character?**

▶ **What kind of animal is it? Can it talk?**

PREVIEW AND PREDICT

Read the title, *Mouse Mess,* and ask:

▶ **What do you think the story is about?**

Share the Read Aloud

FOCUS ON VOCABULARY

Many sentences in the story begin with wonderful onomatopoeic words. Encourage children to listen for these special sound words as you turn each page.

• Invite children to find the object in each illustration that makes that sound.

• Have them predict what the mouse will make a mess of next.

Mouse Mess

Respond to the Literature

TALK ABOUT IT

Share Personal Responses Give children time to laugh at the story and look at the illustrations again.

▶ Was the story fun to listen to?

▶ Were you worried that the mouse might get caught?

▶ Which snack do you think sounded the best?

THINK ABOUT IT

Focus on Plot Invite children to tell how the mouse made the mess.

▶ Why do you think the mouse didn't clean up after itself?

▶ What do you think the family thought when they saw the mess the next morning?

▶ What would you tell the mouse to do next time?

MODIFY Instruction

GIFTED & TALENTED

✳ Review the onomatopoeic words used in *Mouse Mess.* Record on a chart each sound word and the object to which it refers. Then challenge children to name as many other sound words as they can. List them and the objects that make those sounds on the chart. (Examples: *pitter-pat—rain; ding-dong—doorbell; tick-tock—clock*) **(GRAPHIC DEVICE)**

TEACHER TIP

Review the concept of rhyming words before asking children to provide rhyming words in *Mouse Mess*. Use simple examples such as *can* and *fan*, or *hot* and *pot*.

MODIFY Instruction

EXTRA HELP

■ Before children compare the mouse in *Mouse Mess* to a real mouse, you might help them brainstorm a list of words that describe the way mice act or look. Guide children to focus on physical characteristics and behaviors. **(BRAINSTORM)**

Shared Writing

ANIMAL CHARACTER STORY BOOK

Review with children the favorite animal characters they mentioned in the Build Background section.

- As children recall characters, list them on the board or chart paper. Then ask if they like the messy mouse from *Mouse Mess*.

- Have each child fold a piece of construction paper in half. Invite them to draw a picture of an animal character on one half of the paper.

- Then have them label and write about the animal on the other half. Remind them to refer to the list of animal characters for help.

- Bind the pages to make a storybook titled, *Our Animal Friends*.

Repeated Reading

PREDICT RHYMING WORDS

Reread *Mouse Mess*. Pause before saying the last word in each rhyming couplet to let children supply it. Also encourage children to join in by echoing the sound words.

READ AND WRITE INDEPENDENTLY

Journal Place *Mouse Mess* in the Reading Center so that children can read it independently. Also provide science books with photographs of real mice. Have children tell how the pretend mouse in *Mouse Mess* and the real mice in the photographs are alike and how they are different. Children can write about their observations in their Journals.

✅ Comprehension Check

ACT IT OUT

As you reread the story, ask different children to play the role of the mouse and act out each escapade. Encourage children to use sound effects and scurrying movements in their performance.

CENTER WORKSHOPS

Cooking

MATERIALS

- Animal-shaped cookie cutters
- 1 cup flour
- 1/4 cup butter
- 2 ounces shredded cheese
- 1 beaten egg
- Poppy seeds

Animal Crackers

Have fun making animal crackers with the class. Measure the ingredients ahead of time.

- Add the butter to the flour and stir the mixture until it has the texture of bread crumbs. Sift in the cheese and add 2 tablespoons of beaten egg to make a dough. Turn the dough out, knead lightly, and roll it out.
- Invite children to cut out animal shapes from the dough. Place the crackers on baking sheets and brush them with the remaining egg. Sprinkle the crackers with seeds. Bake 12–15 minutes and then let cool.
- Encourage children to make sounds for their animals before they eat them!

Observation: Do children know the names of animal shapes and animal sounds?

Art

MATERIALS

- *Mouse Mess*
- Shoe boxes
- Assorted objects: yarn, buttons, craft sticks, cotton balls, paper cups
- Paste

Make a Mouse House

Reread the first page of *Mouse Mess*, showing children the illustration. Talk together about details in the picture: *What does the mouse use for a bed? Does he have a dresser and a table? What decorations does he have on the wall?* Make sure children realize that everything he has is small, or mouse-sized.

Invite children to use small boxes to make their own houses for the mouse. Encourage them to furnish their houses with small objects. Let them take their projects to the Reading Center to look at when they read *Mouse Mess* independently.

Observation: Notice which children prefer building more than drawing or painting.

DAY 9
OBJECTIVES

CHILDREN WILL:

- generate rhyming words
- review /n/n
- review phonogram *-an*
- review high-frequency words
- read My Book: *It's Playtime!*
- engage in Center Workshops

MATERIALS

- *Big Book of Rhymes and Rhythms,* p. 19
- Sentence Strips for "The Little Nut Tree"
- *Alphabatics*
- My Book: *It's Playtime!*
- My Read and Write Book, p. 11

My Read and Write Book, p. 11

For additional practice see *Scholastic Phonics K,* pp. 75–78. See also Sound and Letter Book: *Nine*

Sounds and Letters

Consonant /n/n

Ⓐ PHONOLOGICAL AWARENESS

Rhyme Tell children that you are going to read aloud a poem from the *Big Book of Rhymes and Rhythms* and ask them to listen for words that begin with /**n**/.

- For fun, give children nuts to hold up each time they hear /**n**/, or simply ask them to stand.
- Then read "The Little Nut Tree" slowly, emphasizing /**n**/ in *nuts, nothing,* and *nutmeg.*
- Invite children to think of words that rhyme with *bear* and *pear.*

Big Book of Rhymes and Rhythms, p. 19

Ⓑ CONCEPTS OF PRINT

Put the *Big Book of Rhymes and Rhythms,* the Sentence Strips for "The Little Nut Tree," and the pocket chart in the Reading Center.

- Read "The Little Nut Tree," asking children to clap on each word.
- Read the rhyme again, placing each Sentence Strip in the pocket chart as you read the line.
- Invite children to frame each word with their fingers. Have them tell when a word begins with the letter *Nn.* Say the words together, emphasizing the sound /**n**/.

> The Little Nut Tree
>
> I had a little nut tree,
>
> Nothing would it bear
>
> But a silver nutmeg
>
> And a golden pear.

EXTRA HELP

■ Some children may confuse the letters *Mm* and *Nn*. Provide tactile experiences for these children using manipulatives such as sandpaper letters. As children say words that begin with *Mm* or *Nn*, have them trace the sandpaper letters with their fingers. Alternatively, cut out *Mm* and *Nn* using a different color for each letter. Observing contrasting colors may help children learn to distinguish the shapes. **(KINESTHETIC)**

C CONNECT SOUND-SPELLING

Alphabetic Principle Page through *Alphabatics* chanting the ABC Song. Stop on the page for *Nn*. Remind children that the letter *Nn* stands for the sound that they hear at the beginning of *nest: n-n-n-nest*. Invite children to say the word with you. You may also want to show the **/n/n** pages for other ABC books children have read this year.

ABC Book Explain to children that they are going to make a new page for their own ABC book. Have children suggest animals, objects, and people whose names begin with **/n/.** When the list is complete, invite children to work together to create the **Nn** page for their ABC Books.

Make an -an Fan Write the phonogram *-an* on the chalkboard. Remind children that *-an* stands for **/an/** as in *man*. Write *_an* on the chalkboard, add the letters **m, c, d,** and **f,** and have children blend the words formed. Model blending as necessary.

Have children fold a piece of paper into a fan and write an *-an* word on each fold.

D VOCABULARY: HIGH-FREQUENCY WORDS

Write the sentence stem *We can go to the* _____ on the chalkboard. Then do the following:

- Have volunteers read the high-frequency words. If necessary, review the read-spell-write routine for each word.
- Invite partners to cut out from magazines pictures of places they would like to go. Then paste them on paper.
- Have children write *We can go to the* at the top of their paper.

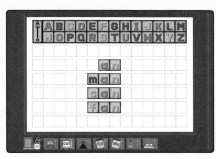

TECHNOLOGY

 Children can write words with *-an* on the **WiggleWorks Plus** Magnet Board.

- Begin with *-an.* Have children use initial **m, c, d,** and **f** to blend new words.

 The rhyme in the *Big Book of Rhymes and Rhythms* is available on the **Sounds of Phonics** audiocassette.

IT'S PLAYTIME!

by Don L. Curry
Illustrated by Mavis Smith

SCHOLASTIC

It's Playtime!

MODIFY Instruction

ESL/ELD

▲ Make sure children understand which sound each word refers to. For example, make sure they understand that *honk* is the sound a horn makes. If possible, bring real toys to class for the demonstration. Then invite children to share the words in their native language that are used to represent each of the sounds. **(MAKE CONNECTIONS)**

Read My Book

INTRODUCE THE BOOK

Let children know that they are going to get their own book that they can read on their own and take home.

▶ **What toys do you play with?**

▶ **Are you quiet or noisy when you play with toys? What kinds of sounds do you make? Why do you do this?**

PREVIEW AND PREDICT

Pass out copies of *It's Playtime!* Read the title, author's name, and illustrator's name. Ask children about the illustration on the cover.

▶ **What is the little girl doing?**

▶ **What might this book be about?**

READ TOGETHER

Read the My Book with children, tracking the print as you read. Guide children to read along in their copies. Point out the sound words and make the noises together.

PHONICS

Ask children to say the word *dolls* aloud.

▶ **What letter stands for the sound you hear at the beginning of the word?**

Encourage children to use other sound-spellings they have learned to help decode words.

READ AND WRITE INDEPENDENTLY

Journal Encourage children to read *It's Playtime!* on their own or in small groups. Provide crayons and invite children to color the illustrations.

HOME/SCHOOL CONNECTION

 Children can take home their My Book to share with family members. Suggest that they add more dialogue to the speech balloon on the last page together.

CENTER
WORKSHOPS

Science

MATERIALS

- Small paper bags
- Small objects whose names begin with *Nn*, such as nickels, noodles, nuts, napkins, and numerals

Nn Nests

Talk about things that birds use to make nests. You may wish to show pictures of different types of nests. Then give small paper bags to children. Take a walk and let them collect things that a bird might use to make a nest. Items might include leaves, grass, string, and twigs. After you return, help children fold down the sides of their bags to make a nest.

When the nests are complete, invite children to participate in a scavenger hunt. Have them search for objects whose names begin with /n/. Encourage children to fill up their nests with their treasures.

Observation: Notice which children recognize the sound for *Nn*.

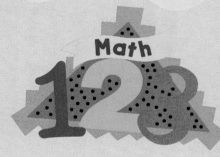

Math

MATERIALS

- Paper
- Pencils
- Markers

My Number Book

Place blank paper in the Math Center and invite children to make number books. Ask them to think of numbers that tell something about themselves, such as their age, birth date, height, telephone number, or bedtime hour. Then encourage children to work with a partner to write their numbers. When they are done writing, have them illustrate their number books and create a title page.

Observation: What numerals do children know how to write?

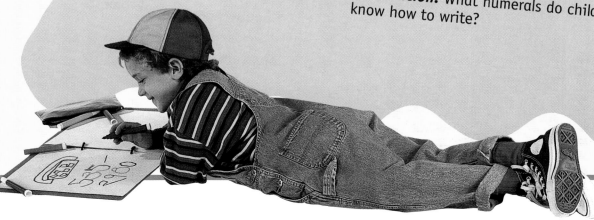

CHILDREN WILL:

- compare and contrast the books they've shared
- listen to a poem
- participate in writing a group chart
- orally blend word parts
- isolate and identify beginning sounds
- create a final project

MATERIALS

- *Listen to the Desert/Oye al desierto*
- *A-Hunting We Will Go!*
- *Let's Get the Rhythm*
- *Mouse Mess*

TECHNOLOGY

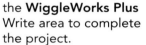

Encourage children to use the drawing and writing tools in the **WiggleWorks Plus** Write area to complete the project.

Put It All Together

Sum It Up

FOCUS ON SOUNDS

Remind children that they have been reading and talking about different sounds. Encourage them to continue noticing sounds and how they are made.

ORAL LANGUAGE: POEM

Read the poem "Little Black Bug" with children. Discuss the rhyming pattern: *rug/bug, high/fly, house/mouse*. Then invite children to make up new verses for the poem.

▶ **Where might a frog have been? What might it say?** *(frog in a log; ribbit)*

Little Black Bug

Little black bug, Little black bug,

Where have you been?

I've been under the rug.

Said little black bug.

Little green fly, Little green fly,

Where have you been?

I've been way up high.

Said little green fly.

Bzzzzzzzzzzzzzzzzzzzz.

Little Old Mouse, Little Old Mouse,

Where have you been?

I've been all through the house.

Said little old mouse.

Squeak-eak-eak-eak-eak.

Margaret Wise Brown

Language Experience Chart

COMPARE AND CONTRAST CHART

Display the books that children have read during the past nine days. Encourage children to recall their impressions of the books. Respond to any questions they may have.

• Create a language chart titled "We Tell Stories With Words and Sounds." Encourage children to talk about the sounds and plots in each of the books you have read together. Write their summaries on the language chart, which might look like the one shown.

We Tell Stories With Words and Sounds

Listen to the Desert	A-Hunting We Will Go!	Let's Get the Rhythm	Mouse Mess
The author describes the sounds you can hear in the desert. She tells the sound words in English and Spanish.	The author tells a story about going to bed. You sing the words to music.	The author tells about a game in which you show rhythm by making sounds with different parts of your body.	The author describes how a mouse makes a mess and the sounds it makes when he is eating dinner.

Observation:

Listen as children associate sounds with letters. Are they using what they know to read sound words?

Watch as children act out scenes. Are they comfortable expressing themselves in front of others?

Listen as children talk about the stories. Are they using sound words to tell about stories?

TEACHER TIP

If children have difficulty isolating the beginning sounds in this activity, emphasize and extend these sounds while stating the object names. You might use a tagboard arrow and point to the beginning to highlight when the beginning sound is being emphasized.

PHONOLOGICAL AWARENESS ASSESSMENT

Begin assessing children's phonological awareness abilities. A phonological awareness assessment is available in the *Assessment Handbook.* See also *Scholastic Phonemic Awareness Kit.*

DAILY PHONICS

Maintenance

Ⓐ PHONOLOGICAL AWARENESS

Animal Blend Tell children you are thinking of an animal. Explain that you will say the first sound in the animal's name and then the rest of the name. Ask children to name the animal.

/m/...ouse	/b/...ear	/n/...ewt
/d/...og	/h/...orse	/f/...ish
/l/...ion	/f/...ox	/g/...oat

You may want to do this again using a different word category such as "Things in the Classroom."

Ⓑ PHONICS ACTIVITY

Make a Mouse Mess Invite children to find a classroom object. Have them put their objects in a pile to make a "Mouse Mess Pile." On chart paper, make a column for each letter of the alphabet.

• Pick up the objects one-by-one. Have children say its name emphasizing the beginning sound.

• Have volunteers name the beginning letter.

• Write the word under the correct column in the alphabet chart.

• To review **/m/m** and **/n/n,** highlight the columns labeled M and N. If there are no words in these columns, have children suggest some.

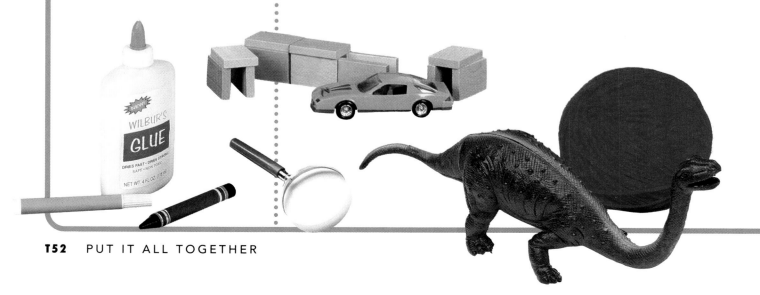

WEEKS 1 AND 2
PROJECT

"Animals Say Hello" Big Book

Throughout the first two weeks, children explored stories told with sounds and words. For the Project following week two of this unit, children can create their own story with sounds and words, making a big book and audiocassette. For the project following week four, children will create a new ending for a story they've read, and act it out with sounds and movements. For the Final Project, children will create a book called "Meet the Authors" to celebrate themselves and their creativity.

MATERIALS

- **Animal pictures**
- **Chart paper**
- **Markers**
- **Crayons**
- **Tape recorder**

BENCHMARKS

Monitor children's progress. Are they

- comparing different stories they've read?
- recognizing how the stories relate to the theme?
- expressing themselves clearly as they talk about stories?

Collect pictures of animals. Pick two pictures and ask children to pretend that one of the animals saw the other and said "hello."

▶ **How does a cat say "hello"? How can we write that sound?**

▶ **Write the animal's name and sound in a sentence on chart paper.**

   The cat sees the cow and says "meow."

- Have the other animal say hello. Ask children what it would say. Pick another animal for it to greet. Write the next line of the story on a separate page.

   The cow sees the horse and says "moo."

- Continue to have children pick animals and think of the sounds that they make. Have them add a new page to the book for each animal using the same sentence structure.

- Form cooperative groups. Have each group illustrate some of the pages, and ask one group to draw a cover. List the children on the cover as the authors and illustrators, and staple the pages together.

- Make an audiocassette of the big book by tape recording as you read the story together. Encourage children to make each animal's sound.

WEEKS
3 AND 4

Kindergarten Goals
for Weeks 3 and 4

Oral Language/ Vocabulary

- participating in rhymes, songs, conversations, and discussions
- participating in choral reading
- discussing pets, farm animals, songs, and building names
- exploring story vocabulary

Reading

- building alphabetic knowledge
- participating in shared reading
- engaging in emergent reading
- exploring concepts of print
- investigating cause/effect
- sequencing story events
- making predictions
- investigating picture details
- tracking print
- comparing/contrasting
- recognizing dialogue
- making inferences
- reading high-frequency words

Writing

- drawing and labeling letter pictures
- making a tally of favorite songs
- writing letters: *Oo, Pp*
- creating a new story page
- completing sentences
- engaging in shared writing
- writing independently in Journals

Listening/Speaking/ Viewing

- listening responsively to stories and other texts read aloud
- identifying chants and rhythm
- developing phonological awareness
- retelling a story
- presenting dramatic interpretations of stories
- contributing to group discussions
- relating personal experiences to literature
- demonstrating visual literacy

Daily Phonics: *Oo* and *Pp*

- reciting classic poems, songs, and nursery rhymes
- naming and recognizing the letters
- recognizing sound/letter relationships
- generating words with /o/, /p/
- decoding words using /o/*o*, /p/*p*
- blending words with *-op*

Center Workshops and Project

- acquiring world knowledge through cross-curricular activities
- creating, planning, and performing new story endings

WEEKS 3 AND 4 RESOURCES

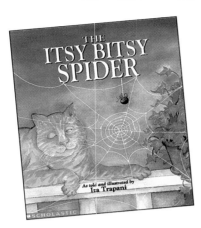

Big Book
Meet the Illustrator
Iza Trapani believes there is a connection between the language and the illustrations in picture books. She always tries to include humor in her books.

Available as audiocassette

Big Book of Rhymes and Rhythms
For teaching phonological awareness, the alphabet, and concepts of print.

• "Polly, Put the Kettle On"
• "Pease Porridge"

Available as audiocassette

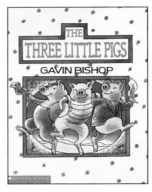

Read Aloud
Meet the Illustrator
Gavin Bishop teaches high school art in New Zealand. Several of his picture books have received international acclaim, and one book, *Mr. Fox,* was named the New Zealand Children's Picture Book of the Year in 1983.

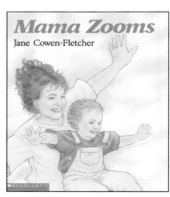

Read Aloud
Meet the Author/ Illustrator
Jane Cowen-Fletcher is a commercial artist. This is her first book and was inspired by her sister, a veterinarian and mother, who was left paraplegic after an accident. She has since written *It Takes a Village.*

ABC Book
Meet the Author/ Illustrator
Suse MacDonald got the idea for *Alphabatics* in art school while taking a topography course. It took her many years to convince the publisher to print *Alphabatics.*

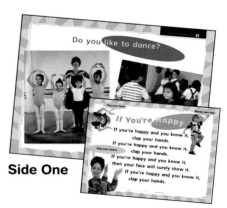
Side One

Side Two

SourceCard
• Do you like to dance?
• "If You're Happy"

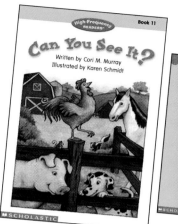

High-Frequency Reader

My Read and Write Book

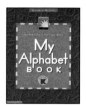

My Alphabet Book

ESL/ELD Teaching Guide

My Books

To take home to share.

Introducing the Mentor

Pat Mora enjoys acting out stories as well as writing them. She uses words, sounds, and movements to tell her stories, just like kindergartners do!

DAYS AT A GLANCE

WEEKS 3 AND 4

	Daily Phonics	Literature	Shared Writing	Workshops and Projects
DAY 1	Phonological Awareness: Oral Segmentation Review /l/l, /m/m, /n/n	*Alphabatics* by Suse MacDonald [ABC BOOK]	Draw and Label Letter Pictures	Science: Watch It Change! Cooking: *Aa* to *Zz* Pretzels
DAY 2	**Vowel /o/o** Phonological Awareness: Oral Segmentation	*The Itsy Bitsy Spider* by Iza Trapani [BIG BOOK·LITTLE BOOK] **High-Frequency Reader:** *Can You See It?*	Make a Tally of Favorite Songs	Science: Animals in the Neighborhood Math: Measure How Far
DAY 3	**Vowel /o/o** Phonological Awareness: Alliteration Introduce Sound-Spelling	*The Itsy Bitsy Spider* by Iza Trapani [BIG BOOK·LITTLE BOOK]	Concepts of Print: Tracking Print Write *Oo* Make a Bulletin Board	Science: Research Spiders Science: Experiment with Spouts!
DAY 4	**Vowel /o/o** Phonological Awareness: Oral Blending Review Sound-Spelling	*The Three Little Pigs* by Gavin Bishop [READ ALOUD]	Focus on Repetitive Language	Art: Build a Fine House Games: This Little Piggy
DAY 5	**Vowel /o/o** Phonological Awareness: Oral Segmentation Maintain Sound-Spelling	"Polly, Put the Kettle On" a rhyme *Alphabatics* **My Book:** *I Run*	Concepts of Print: Commas High-Frequency Word: *it*	Music & Movement: Around the *O* We Go Alphabet: *Oo* Is for Opposite

	Daily Phonics	Literature	Shared Writing	Workshops and Projects
DAY 6	**Consonant /p/p** Phonological Awareness: Oral Segmentation	*Clifford the Big Red Dog* by Norman Bridwell	Add a Page	Art: A Toy for Clifford Math: How Big is Clifford?
DAY 7	**Consonant /p/p** Phonological Awareness: Auditory Discrimination Introduce Sound-Spelling	**SourceCard** Do You Like To Dance? "If You're Happy" **High-Frequency Reader:** *Can You See It?*	Create New Verses Write *Pp*	Music & Movement: Weather Dances Social Studies: A Collage of Feelings
DAY 8	**Consonant /p/p** Phonological Awareness: Oral Blending Review Sound-Spelling Phonogram *-op*	*Mama Zooms* by Jane Cowen-Fletcher	Finish the Sentence	Science: Zooming Art: Our Imagination Book
DAY 9	**Consonant /p/p** Phonological Awareness: Auditory Discrimination Maintain Sound-Spelling	"Pease Porridge" a nursery rhyme *Mama Zooms* **My Book:** *My Name Is Sam*	Concepts of Print: Connect Spoken and Written Words High-Frequency Words	Music & Movement: Calling All Songwriters Cooking: *Pp*'s are Popping
DAY 10	Phonological Awareness: Oral Segmentation Phonics Maintenance	**Review Books from Weeks 3 and 4**	Make a Compare and Contrast Chart	Project: Create, Plan, and Perform "The Three Little Pigs"

CHILDREN WILL:

- differentiate sound positions
- review consonants /l/l, /m/m, /n/n
- recognize *Oo* and *Pp*
- discuss letter shapes
- read *Alphabatics*
- label pictures with letters
- engage in Center Workshops

MATERIALS

- *Alphabatics*
- Old magazines and catalogs
- Picture Cards, R33–34

GUIDED READING

To conclude each day's reading session, meet with guided reading groups. You might use Scholastic's Guided Reading Library or other books in your library.

TECHNOLOGY

Children can get more practice with identifying letters at **www.funschool.com**. The site offers educational games designed for kindergarten.

Share the ABC Book

DAILY PHONICS

Warm-Up: Wordplay

Ⓐ PHONOLOGICAL AWARENESS

Oral Segmentation: Beginning or Ending? Show the following picture cards: *nose, sun, nut, pan, nest, man, ten, pen*. Have children name each picture. If the picture name begins with **/n/n,** have children put it in one pile. If the picture name ends with **/n/n,** have them put it in another pile.

Invite children to look at the two piles to review the words and the beginning and ending sounds.

Ⓑ PHONICS MAINTENANCE

Review Consonants /l/l, /m/m, /n/n Invite children to sing the alphabet song as you page through *Alphabatics*. On the pages for *l, m,* and *n,* ask children to say the sound that each letter stands for and to name the objects pictured. Invite children to think of other words for each sound.

Build Background

ORAL LANGUAGE: CHANGE IT!
Letter Drawing Game Write a letter on a piece of chart paper. Ask the children to think of the shape of the letter.

▶ **Can you think of other things shaped like this?**

Ask for a volunteer to come up and make it into a picture. Invite children to name and label the objects they draw.

PREVIEW AND PREDICT
Show children the cover of *Alphabatics,* reviewing the title and the author/illustrator's name. Encourage children to try to recall some of the objects pictured in the book.

▶ **Do you think we will see any of the pictures we drew?**

SET A PURPOSE
Ask children what two letters follow *m* and *n.* Point out that they will now be learning about *o* and *p.*

▶ **What do you think is on the *Oo* and *Pp* pages?**

Read the ABC Book

ALPHABETIC KNOWLEDGE: *Oo* **AND** *Pp*

Read the book aloud. After each page, ask children what the next letter will be. Invite them to try to recall what the letter turns into. You might use the ABC Cards in your classroom to remind them of the sequence and the shape of each letter.

▶ **Which letter will be next?**

▶ **Think of the shape of that letter. What could it turn into?**

When you reach the pages for *Oo* and *Pp,* have children stop and notice the uppercase and lowercase forms of the letter. Say the name of the letters together.

Alphabatics

Respond to the Literature

TALK ABOUT IT

Share Personal Responses Encourage children to share comments and ask questions about the ABC Book.

▶ **Which is your favorite page? Why?**

▶ **What happened to the letter that begins your name?**

Turn to the *Oo* page.

▶ **What part of the owl did the *o* become?**

▶ **What other things are shaped like an *Oo*?**

Repeat with the picture on the *Pp* page.

THINK ABOUT IT

Focus on Letter Shapes Invite children to look around the room for objects that remind them of a letter in the alphabet. Write down their observations on chart paper. You might get them started with these observations:

• I see an *Ll* at the edge of the door.

• I see an *Oo* in the bubbles in the fish tank.

• I see an *I* in the table leg.

• I see an *A* in the doll house roof.

GIFTED & TALENTED

✴ Invite small groups to choose favorite letters of the alphabet. Have them find and label all the objects in the room whose names begin with that letter. (MAKE CONNECTIONS)

Shared Writing

LABEL LETTER COLLAGES

Ask each child to choose a letter from the alphabet.

- Invite children to look through old magazines and catalogs to find objects with names that begin with the sound of the letter they chose.

- Have children cut out the objects they find and glue them to a piece of paper.

- Then help each child label their collage by writing the letter he or she chose.

- Encourage them to label the individual pictures using the letters that they know.

WRITE MESSAGES

Display children's drawings for all to enjoy. Encourage children to draw or write a simple note to tell a classmate that they like their drawing. Suggest that they draw a smile face or write *nice* on a sticky note which they can attach to the drawing.

Repeated Reading

JOIN IN!

Reread the ABC Book with children. Invite them to join in as you read the letter names and labels.

READ AND WRITE INDEPENDENTLY

Journal Place several copies of *Alphabatics* in the Reading Center for children to read independently or with a partner. Encourage them to write in their Journal about their favorite letter pages.

Comprehension Check

ACT IT OUT

As you reread the story, children can make the shapes of the letters with their hands or their bodies. Some children may wish to act out both cases of the letters. Invite children to turn into and act out the objects or animals on the page.

CENTER WORKSHOPS

Watch It Change!

Children can create a page for a class ABC book. Have partners choose a letter and think about what animal or object it can be turned into. Together, you might flip through *Alphabatics* to get some ideas. List suggestions on chart paper. Some ideas might include changing *C* into the handle of a cup, or *M* into a mountain.

Encourage children to use a variety of materials to create their page. When children are finished, invite them to share their work. Pages can be bound together to create a class ABC book.

Observation: What materials do children use to create their letter transformations?

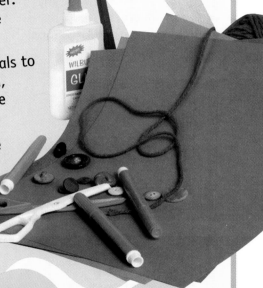

MATERIALS

- *Alphabatics*
- Construction paper
- Variety of art materials such as tissue paper, buttons, yarn
- Markers or crayons

Aa to Zz Pretzels

Help children prepare the pretzel dough. Dissolve the yeast in cold water. Add flour, salt, and sugar. Mix, adding flour if needed so the dough is not sticky.

Write the alphabet on a chart where children can see the letters. Ask each child to roll the dough to form the letters *Oo* and *Pp*. Guide children to choose other letters from the alphabet to form with the dough.

Place letter pretzels on a cookie sheet to bake at 425 degrees for 12–15 minutes. Let children name and trace the letters.

Observation: How do children form the letters with the dough?

MATERIALS

- 1 package dry yeast
- 1 1/2 cups cold water
- 4 cups flour
- 1 teaspoon sugar
- 1 teaspoon salt

Share the Big Book

DAY 2 OBJECTIVES

CHILDREN WILL:

- recognize /o/
- read and respond to *The Itsy Bitsy Spider*
- discuss favorite nursery songs
- compare/contrast song versions
- participate in making a tally of favorite songs
- engage in Center Workshops

MATERIALS

- *The Itsy Bitsy Spider*
- My Read and Write Book, p. 12

The Big Book is available on audiocassette in the Literacy Place Listening Center.

DAILY PHONICS

Vowel /o/o

PHONOLOGICAL AWARENESS

Oral Segmentation: Beginning Sounds Invite children to join in as you sing this repetitive song. After singing, repeat the phrase "And on . . ." isolating the beginning /o/ in the word *on; o-o-on.*

The Green Grass Grows All Around

1. There was a tree (echo)
All in the wood, (echo)
The prettiest little tree, (echo)
That you ever did see, (echo)
The tree in a hole and the hole in the ground
And the green grass grew all around, all around, and the green grass grew all around.
2. And on that tree . . .There was a limb,
3. And on that limb . . .There was a branch,
4. And on that branch . . .There was a nest,
5. And in that nest . . .There was an egg,
6. And in that egg . . .There was a bird,
7. And on that bird . . .There was a wing,
8. And on that wing . . .There was a feather,

Build Background

ORAL LANGUAGE: FAVORITE NURSERY SONGS

Talk about some of the songs the class sings together.

▶ **What are some of the songs we like to sing? What are some other songs you know?**

Invite children to share their favorite songs. Then explain that some songs, called Nursery Songs, are often sung with young children and many of these songs have been around for a long, long time.

PREVIEW AND PREDICT Display the cover of *The Itsy Bitsy Spider* and read the name of the author/illustrator. Explain that this is a *retelling* of the popular song and that the author added new things to it.

The Itsy Bitsy Spider

▶ **What kind of homes do spiders build?**

▶ **What do you think the cat on the cover will do?**

▶ **How do you think this book will be different from the song?**

Read the Big Book

LOOK FOR PICTURE CLUES Before beginning the first verse, ask children if they know how a water spout works. If necessary, explain that it brings rainwater from the roof down to the ground. Then read or sing the story aloud. Before you start a new verse, ask children to look for a picture clue that might tell them where the spider will climb next.

Respond to the Literature

TALK ABOUT IT **Share Personal Responses** Encourage children to talk about their reactions to the story.

▶ **Which is your favorite verse? Why?**

▶ **What do you think the spider was trying to do each time it climbed something?**

▶ **How do you feel when you try to do something but keep getting stopped?**

ESL/ELD

▲ As you read or sing the story aloud, track the print with your hand to encourage children to follow along. During the follow-up discussion, point to the pictures and prompt children to repeat key words. **(MODEL)**

THINK ABOUT IT **Explore Character's Feelings** Discuss with children that we can often tell how someone is feeling by looking at the expression on their face. Look back through the book with the children. Ask them to notice and comment on the different expressions on the spider's face.

▶ **How do you think the spider felt each time it had to try again?**

▶ **Why do you think the spider didn't give up trying to spin a web?**

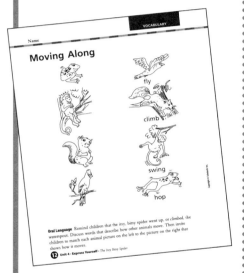

My Read and Write Book, p. 12

Shared Writing

MAKE A TALLY OF FAVORITE SONGS

Invite children to make a tally of their favorite songs.

• Write the favorite songs they suggest on chart paper. Have children name the letters as you write each word.

• After song titles are written, read them again and ask children to vote for their favorite.

• Count votes and demonstrate for children how to make tally marks next to each song title.

• After all votes are in, count up the tally marks. Stress the fifth mark each time, creating a rhythm for counting.

Each child can illustrate and label a page depicting their favorite song. Then bind the pages into a class book titled "Our Favorite Songs."

Repeated Reading

COMPARE/ CONTRAST VERSIONS

Reread the Big Book, inviting children to chime in as they become familiar with the pattern of the text. Ask children to listen for all the different things that happen to the spider in this version of the song.

When you finish reading, ask children what happens at the end of the version of the song with which they are familiar. You may refer back to *Creative Expression* SourceCard #1.

READ AND WRITE INDEPENDENTLY

Journal Place copies of *The Itsy Bitsy Spider* in the Reading Center so that children can enjoy it on their own or in small groups. Have them write about their favorite place that the spider climbed.

☑ Comprehension Check

ACT IT OUT

As you sing the story aloud, encourage children to act out each verse, inviting them to make climbing movements and to use facial expressions to show feeling.

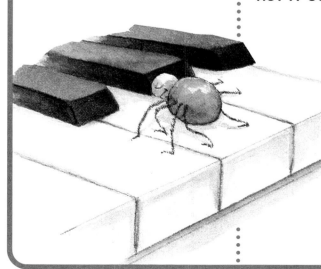

CENTER WORKSHOPS

Science

Animals in the Neighborhood

Take children on a walk around the schoolyard or neighborhood to look for signs of animal life. Before you leave for the walk, help children make a list of what they think they might see. When you return to school, ask children to recall all the animals they saw on their walk. Then revisit the original list to check children's predictions. Help children determine if the animals they saw were wild animals or pets.

Each child can illustrate and label something they saw on the walk. Then bind the pages into a class book titled *Neighborhood Animals*.

Observation: Notice how attentive children are to the prints, nests, and animals they see outdoors.

MATERIALS

- *The Itsy Bitsy Spider*
- Drawing paper
- Pencils, markers, or crayons
- Stapler

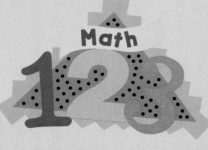

Math

Measure How Far

Point out that some spiders are about the same size as a connecting cube! Ask each child to measure with cubes, how far it would be for a spider to climb two classroom objects such as a wastebasket, a boot, or a desk. List choices on chart paper.

Show children how to measure the distance between the floor and the seat of a chair. Then count the number of cubes in the stack.

Have children use the cubes to measure the objects they chose. Then help them record their measurements on the chart. When the class is finished, have children compare the different lengths and suggest which items would take the spider the longest and shortest amount of time to climb.

Observation: Notice how children record their measurement.

MATERIALS

- Connecting cubes
- Clipboard or cardboard
- Drawing paper
- Pencils or markers

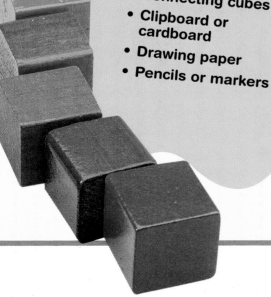

Revisit the Big Book

DAY 3 OBJECTIVES

CHILDREN WILL:

- listen for alliteration
- recognize vowel /o/o
- write *Oo*
- reread *The Itsy Bitsy Spider*
- explore concepts of print: directionality
- identify the high-frequency word *it*
- engage in Center Workshops

MATERIALS

- *The Itsy Bitsy Spider*
- **High-Frequency Reader:** *Can You See It?*
- *Alphabatics*
- **My Alphabet Book, p. 17**
- **My Read and Write Book, p. 13**
- **ABC Card: Oo**

The Big Book is available on audiocassette in the Literacy Place Listening Center.

My Alphabet Book, p. 17

Vowel /o/o

A PHONOLOGICAL AWARENESS

Alliteration Write the following silly sentence on the chalkboard. Say it aloud stressing the **/o/** sound.

Oliver Octopus rode on an ox.

Read the sentence again, having children clap whenever they hear the **/o/** sound. Invite them to read the sentence, emphasizing each initial **/o/** sound.

B CONNECT SOUND-SPELLING

Introduce Vowel /o/o Point to the silly sentence on the chalkboard. Read it aloud indicating the letter *o* at the beginning of *Oliver, Octopus, on,* and *ox*. Tell children that this letter stands for /o/ as in *Octopus*. Display the ABC card for ***Oo,*** if available. Have children say the word *octopus* aloud. Indicate the letters ***Oo***.

Letter Formation

WRITE THE LETTER

Write *Oo* on the chalkboard. Point out the capital and small forms of the letter. Model how to write the letter using the rhyme provided below.

- Have children write both forms of the letter in the air with their fingers. Ask children to make the letter's sound as they practice writing.

Oo

The popcorn pops, hot! hot! hot!
But stays inside this big, round, pot.
(Circle all the way around.)

Reread the Big Book

OPTIONS

Causes and Effects Reread the book, guiding children to discuss the reasons for the events in each verse. Ask questions such as:

The Itsy Bitsy Spider

▶ **The waterspout was dry when the spider began to climb. What happened to make her fall? When did she try to climb the spout again?**

▶ **Why did the spider fall off the kitchen wall? What happened so she could try again?**

▶ **What made the spider fall off the pail? Was the mouse still in the room when she tried again?**

Decoding Strategies Point out that children can use the letters and sounds they have learned to figure out words. Stop on the page that begins *Swoosh! went the fan.*

Read the first three words. Then help children use their knowledge of **/f/f** and the phonogram **-an** to blend the word *fan.*

Encourage children to use other sound-spellings to help decode words.

READ AND WRITE INDEPENDENTLY

Journal Encourage children to read *The Itsy Bitsy Spider* on their own or in small groups. Invite them to draw and write their own new episodes in their Journals.

MODIFY Instruction

ESL/ELD

▲ English language learners may enjoy pantomiming the actions in the story. Show them hand signs and actions to convey the meaning of the words. Then pantomime again and have them say the words the actions refer to. **(PANTOMIME)**

Concepts of Print

TRACKING PRINT

Display the first page of *The Itsy Bitsy Spider.* Ask a volunteer to show you where you should begin reading.

• As you read the first line, track the print from left to right. Then sweep down and to the left to read the second line.

• After reading the first sentence, turn the page and invite a volunteer to come up and track the print with his or her index finger.

• Continue until all volunteers have had a chance to track the print. Guide children as necessary to follow the left-to-right and top-to-bottom movements.

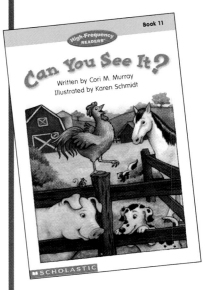

Can You See It?

My Read and Write Book, p. 13

Read High-Frequency Reader

INTRODUCE THE BOOK

Show the book *Can You See It?* Read the title and the author's name. Explain that each page shows a part of an animal and asks the question, "Can you see it?"

▶ **Where do you think this story takes place? What animals do you think you might see in this book?**

HIGH-FREQUENCY WORD: it

On the board, write the sentence *Can you see it?* Review the high-frequency words: *I, can, you,* and *see.* Underline the word *it.* Then write *it* on a note card. Read it aloud.

• Display the card and have children read the word.

• Help children spell it aloud, clapping on each letter.

• Ask children to write it in the air as they state aloud each letter.

Next write the sentence *I can see it.* Play a game by naming something in the classroom that you can see. If children can see it too, have them come up to the board and read the sentence *I can see it,* pointing to each word.

Add the card for *it* to the Word Wall.

SHARE THE HIGH-FREQUENCY READER

Read the story aloud, tracking the print. Invite children to point to the high-frequency word *it.*

• After each two-page spread ask: *Can you see the animals that the children see?* Encourage children to share experiences when they actually saw the animals mentioned in the book.

SHARED WRITING

Invite children to help make a bulletin board called *Can You See It?*

• Have children draw an animal. Then give them another piece of paper and have them write: *Can you see it?*

• Help children cover part of their drawing by attaching the paper on which they wrote *Can you see it?*

• Display the pictures and have the class guess what animal is partially hidden.

CENTER WORKSHOPS

Science

MATERIALS

- Books about spiders
- Chart paper

Research Spiders

Make a KWL Chart labeled *Spiders*. Ask children to share their knowledge about spiders. Then invite them to generate questions they have about spiders. Fill in the chart.

Take children to the library. Talk about where to find information. As you look through the books, explain the Table of Contents and other features.

After you have finished your research, fill in the chart with everything you learned about spiders.

Observation: What kinds of questions do children generate?

SPIDERS

What we know:
Spiders spin webs.
Spiders have 8 legs.

What we want to find out:
Do spiders lay eggs?
Why do spiders spin webs?

What we learned:
Spiders do lay eggs.

Science

MATERIALS

- Tin foil
- Paper towel rolls
- Kitchen funnels
- Sand or water
- A sand or water table, or large plastic tub placed on a low table

Experiment With Spouts!

Set up a sand or water table. Provide paper towel rolls (if sand is used) and kitchen funnels.

Talk about the waterspout in *The Itsy Bitsy Spider*. Discuss the shape of a spout and how it is used.

Invite children to use tin foil to create their own spouts. Then encourage them to compare their spouts with others. Through which spouts does the water (sand) come out of more quickly?

At another time, invite children to experiment with other materials such as bird seed or rice.

Observation: How do children form their spout? What kinds of comparisons do they make?

DAY 4 OBJECTIVES

CHILDREN WILL:

- orally blend word parts
- review vowel /o/o
- discuss building
- read and respond to *The Three Little Pigs*
- sequence the story
- retell the story
- engage in Center Workshops

MATERIALS

- *The Three Little Pigs*
- My Read and Write Book, p. 14

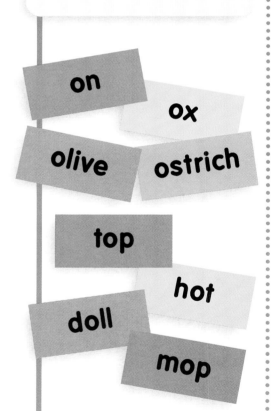

TECHNOLOGY

 Children might enjoy watching another version of *The Three Little Pigs*. James Marshall's retelling of the story is available on video from Weston Woods.

Share the Read Aloud

Vowel /o/o

A PHONOLOGICAL AWARENESS

Oral Blending State aloud the following word parts, and ask children to blend them to make a whole word. Provide corrective feedback and modeling when necessary.

/m/. . . op	/p/. . . ot	/d/. . . oll
/s/. . . ock	/h/. . . op	/g/. . . ot

Help children to notice that the **/o/** sound is in the middle of these words.

B CONNECT SOUND-SPELLING

An Armful of *Oo*'s Remind children that the letter ***o*** stands for **/o/** as in ***octopus.*** Draw and label an octopus on chart paper. On index cards write the words *on, ox, olive, ostrich, top, hot, doll,* and *mop.*

Tell children the octopus will hold on one side four words that have **/o/** at the beginning of the word. On the other side it will hold four words that have **/o/** in the middle. Read each word. Invite children to look at the card and attach it to an octopus arm on the correct side.

Build Background

ORAL LANGUAGE: BUILDING

Ask children to think about different kinds of buildings.

▶ **What kinds of materials are used for building? What tools do people use to build?**

▶ **What materials make a building strong?**

PREVIEW AND PREDICT

Show the cover of *The Three Little Pigs*. Read the title and author/illustrator's name. Talk about versions of the story they know.

▶ **Why do you think these pigs are dancing?**

Share the Read Aloud

FOCUS ON CHARACTER

As you read, use different voices to create distinct personalities for each of the little pigs. Try to capture the sly wolf's wheedling tone as he attempts to convince the little pigs to open their doors or go on an outing.

Ask children about each character as they meet them in the book. Ask questions such as:

► **Would this character make a good friend? How does how he acts and what he says help you know this?**

► **How would you describe this pig (wolf, etc.)? How do they act in the story?**

► **Is the wolf friendly? Do you trust him?**

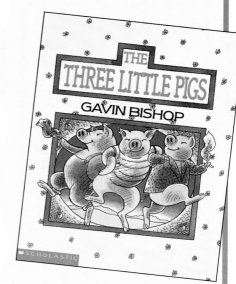

The Three Little Pigs

Respond to the Literature

TALK ABOUT IT

Share Personal Responses Ask children to describe their favorite part of the book. Invite them to check their predictions.

► **Is this version of the story the same as or different from other versions you have heard? What parts are different?**

► **How do you think each pig felt when it heard the wolf at its doors? Why?**

► **What character in the story made the smartest decisions? Why do you think this?**

THINK ABOUT IT

Create Alternative Story Endings Ask children to think about the story ending. Discuss other endings children have heard or imagined for *The Three Little Pigs*.

► **Do you prefer happy endings or sad endings?**

► **What different ending would you like to see for the three little pigs?**

Make a "Happy Endings/Sad Endings" chart. Fill it in with children's story ending ideas. Then encourage them to illustrate their endings.

ESL/ELD

▲ Have English language learners choose one character to "become." Ask questions that require one word answers so they can participate in the Focus on Character discussion. For example:

Are you the Wolf?

Do you have a house of sticks?

What is your name?
(CONTEXT CLUES)

PROFESSIONAL DEVELOPMENT

ADRIA KLEIN

The Importance of Drama

Dramatization can help bring story elements to life. Character's feelings become clearer through dialogue. Plot becomes easier to recognize through pantomime. While creating sets and costumes can make a setting "real."

Stay in Touch

My Read and Write Book, p. 14

Shared Writing

FOCUS ON REPETITIVE LANGUAGE

Encourage children to say the following dialogue with you:

"Little pig, little pig, let me come in."

"No, not by the hair of my chinny, chin chin."

"Then I'll huff and I'll puff and I'll blow your house in."

- Ask children to think of other things that the wolf might do if the pigs do not open their doors.
- Work with children to write the sentence, "I'll huff and I'll puff and I'll blow your house in," replacing the words *huff, puff,* and *blow* with new words that describe different ways for the wolf to behave.
- Encourage children to write the letters that stand for the sounds they know.

Repeated Reading

FOCUS ON DIALOGUE

Divide children into two groups before you begin a rereading of the story. One group can be the voice of the wolf. The other group can be the voices of the pigs.

Guide each group to recite the dialogue that is repeated each time the wolf threatens to blow one of the pig's houses down. Pause when you reach this predictable dialogue. Encourage children to say their lines with expression.

READ AND WRITE INDEPENDENTLY

Journal Place *The Three Little Pigs* in the Reading Center so children can read it independently. Encourage children to draw and write about the story in their Journals.

✅ Comprehension Check

ACT IT OUT

Designate different areas of the classroom as sites for the different scenes in the story. As you reread the story, let children take the parts of the pigs, men, and wolf, and act out each scene in the appropriate area as it takes place.

CENTER WORKSHOPS

Art

Build a Fine House

What kinds of houses can children construct from blocks, sticks, and straw? Invite children to explore these and similar materials to create different types of dwellings.

- If children wish, they can try their own huff-and-puff test to determine the strength of their structures. Before they blow, ask them to predict which house is most likely to remain standing. How does this compare with what happened in the story?

Observation: How involved do children become in this construction project? What material do they use to build?

MATERIALS

- Twigs, hay, straw, and other natural materials
- Corrugated cardboard
- Craft sticks
- Tape and glue
- Clay

Games

This Little Piggy

Children can cut apart egg cartons and use individual cups and string to fashion little pig snouts. Children can cut construction-paper ears for the pigs and wolf, tucking the ears into headbands.

- Encourage groups to wear their costumes as they perform their version of this tale.
- Children can wear their costumes as they imagine and pretend to live a day in the life of a little pig or a big wolf. Place *The Three Little Pigs* in the Dramatic Play Center for children to find out how the pigs and wolf look as they express themselves.

Observation: What story elements do children use in their performances?

MATERIALS

- Construction paper
- Scissors
- Headbands
- Egg cartons
- String
- Dress-up clothes
- *The Three Little Pigs*

CHILDREN WILL:

- orally segment words (beginning sounds)
- review sound-spelling relationship for /o/o
- review high-frequency words
- read My Book: *I Run*
- engage in Center Workshops

MATERIALS

- *Big Book of Rhymes and Rhythms,* p. 20
- Alphabet Card: *Oo*
- Sentence Strips for "Polly Put the Kettle On"
- *The Itsy Bitsy Spider*
- Magnetic letters
- My Read and Write Book, p. 15

My Read and Write Book, p. 15

For additional practice see *Scholastic Phonics K,* pp. 79–82. See also Sound and Letter Book: *Octopus Gets the Olive.*

Sounds and Letters

 DAILY PHONICS

 and Read My Book

Vowel /o/o

Ⓐ **PHONOLOGICAL AWARENESS**

Song Display a small appliance or piece of equipment with an on/off switch. Ask a volunteer to help you demonstrate how to work the switch.

Ask children to say the words *on* and *off*, isolating the beginning sound: *o-o-on*; *o-o-off*. Invite children to repeat and to name the letter that makes that sound.

Read or sing aloud "Polly, Put the Kettle On" from the *Big Book of Rhymes and Rhythms.* Emphasize the initial **/o/** sound in the word *on.* Have children join in during a second reading.

Big Book of Rhymes and Rhythms, p. 20

Ⓑ **CONCEPTS OF PRINT**

Put the *Big Book of Rhymes and Rhythms,* the Sentence Strips for "Polly Put the Kettle On," and a pocket chart in the Reading Center. Then do the following:

- Read "Polly Put the Kettle On," asking children to listen for the parts that repeat.
- Reread the rhyme together. Ask volunteers to place the Sentence Strips in a pocket chart as each line is read.
- Point to the commas after the names *Polly* and *Sukey.*
- Review with children what this punctuation mark means. Read these sentences together, pausing after the comma.

Polly, put the kettle on,

Polly, put the kettle on,

Polly, put the kettle on,

And let's drink tea.

EXTRA HELP

■ Children might identify words that contain the long *o* sound. Acknowledge that the words do contain the letter *o* but that the letter stands for a different sound in those words. Compare the sound of the long *o* word to a short *o* word to help children hear the difference. **(MODEL)**

C CONNECT SOUND-SPELLING

Alphabetic Principle Reread the Sentences Strips for "Polly Put the Kettle On." Stop before you get to the word *on.* Have children identify the first letter and say the sound. Invite children to find other examples of the letter *Oo* in the rhyme. Read each word together.

ABC Book Explain to children that they are going to make a new page for their own ABC book. Have children make suggestions of animals, objects, and people whose names begin with **/o/** as in **on.** You may want to help them by suggesting the following words: *ostrich, olive, ox, octopus, otter.* When the list is complete, invite children to work together to create the **Oo** page for their ABC books.

Finger Paint *Oo's* Provide children with paper and finger paints. Write the letter *Oo* on a chart and invite children to experiment making *Oo's* with the finger paints. Encourage children to think of ***O*** words, and help them add labels to the sides of the chart.

D VOCABULARY: HIGH-FREQUENCY WORDS

Write the sentence *I see it* on the chalkboard. Read the sentence aloud and then do the following:

• Ask a volunteer to come up and point to the high-frequency word *it.* Review the word.

• Ask children to dictate other sentences that include the word *it.* Write these on the board as children say them.

• Read the sentences back to children, pointing to each word as you read.

• Finally, point to each word in the sentences without reading them. Ask children to stand up each time you point to the word *it.*

TECHNOLOGY

The **WiggleWorks Plus** Magnet Board activity pictured here provides additional practice with words that begin with /o/. Ask children to write the words **off** and **on.** Discuss the sound that *Oo* stands for. Invite children to build other words containing the /o/ sound.

The rhyme in the *Big Book of Rhymes and Rhythms* is available on the **Sounds of Phonics** audiocassette.

I Run

ESL/ELD

▲ Have children make a bridge with blocks from the Block Center. Provide a small cardboard box and a stuffed dog. Invite children to use the stuffed dog to demonstrate as you say the following words: *in, out, up, down, over, under.* **(DEMONSTRATE)**

Read My Book

INTRODUCE THE BOOK

Let children know that they are going to get their own book that they can read on their own and take home.

▶ **What are different ways you can move fast?**

PREVIEW AND PREDICT

Pass out copies of *I Run*. Read the title and the author's and illustrator's names. Talk about the cover illustration.

▶ **Is this dog going fast or slow? How can you tell?**

▶ **Why do you think the dog is running?**

READ TOGETHER

Read the My Book with children, tracking the print as you read. Guide children to read along in their copies and to point out all the places the animal runs.

PHONICS

Point to the word *down*.

▶ **What letter is at the beginning of this word? What sound does this letter make?**

Repeat with other sound-spellings children have learned.

READ AND WRITE INDEPENDENTLY

Journal Encourage children to read *I Run* on their own or in small groups. Provide crayons and invite children to color the illustrations. Encourage children to add their own page showing a place they like to run.

HOME/SCHOOL CONNECTION

Children can take home their My Books to share with family members and friends. Suggest that children set up an obstacle course with family members to act out the story of *I Run*.

CENTER WORKSHOPS

Music & Movement

MATERIALS

- **Butcher paper**
- **Marker**
- **Masking tape**

Around the *O* We Go

Cut out a circular piece of butcher paper and make two thick lines around the edge with a marker, about 6 inches apart.

- Tape the *O* on the floor, and ask children to name the letter. Explain that children can try to walk around the *O*, keeping their feet inside the two lines. They don't want to step out of the *O*, or in the *O*.

- Put on some music, and encourage children to test their balance as they go around the *O*.

Observation: Notice how long children try to walk around the *O* without stepping out of the lines.

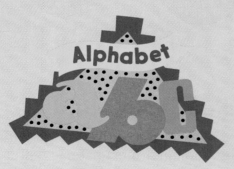

Alphabet

MATERIALS

- **Index cards with simple pairs of opposites written or drawn on them**
- **Common classroom objects to be used for props**

Oo is for Opposite

Prepare for this activity by inviting a child to turn off the classroom lights. Then ask someone to do the opposite. Discuss the idea that the words *on* and *off* are opposites.

- Write the word *opposite* on a chart, and ask children to point out the letter *o*.

- Children can form small groups. Begin by having one volunteer choose a card. Help that child read the words or name the objects drawn on the card. Then the child can pantomime the word or object while the other children try to guess the word and its opposite.

Observation: Notice how children act out the words and figure out each word's opposite.

DAY 6 OBJECTIVES

CHILDREN WILL:

- orally segment words (beginning sounds)
- recognize /p/
- reread *Clifford the Big Red Dog*
- create new pages to go along with the story
- sequence the story
- engage in Center Workshops

MATERIALS

- *Clifford the Big Red Dog*
- *My Read and Write Book*, pp. 16–18

GUIDED READING

To conclude each day's reading session, meet with guided reading groups. You might use Scholastic's Guided Reading Library or other books in your library.

TECHNOLOGY

The book *Clifford the Big Red Dog* mentions many kinds of dogs. Invite children to describe and make an imaginary dog using the Paint tools in the My Book Area. Then they can write about what their dog looks like.

Share the WiggleWorks Book

DAILY PHONICS

Consonant /p/p

PHONOLOGICAL AWARENESS

Oral Segmentation: Beginning Sound Read aloud the title "Pawpaw Patch." Invite children to say the word *pawpaw*, isolating the /p/ sound: *p-p-paw*.

- Then sing the song. Invite children to sing along. Have them clap when they sing the words that begin with the sound /p/.

Pawpaw Patch

Where, oh where, is dear little Peter?
Where, oh where, is dear little Peter?
Where, oh where, is dear little Peter?
Way down yonder in the pawpaw patch.

Build Background

ORAL LANGUAGE: PETS

Encourage children to talk about their pets. Have them discuss caring for a big pet and a little pet.

▶ **How do you care for a big pet? A little pet?**

▶ **Do you think it would cost more to feed a big dog or a little fish?**

PREVIEW AND PREDICT

Show the cover of *Clifford the Big Red Dog*. Invite children to talk about the illustration.

▶ **What is the girl doing?**

▶ **How do you think she feels about Clifford?**

Read the WiggleWorks Book

EXPLORE THE PICTURES

As you read the story, help children see that Emily Elizabeth is telling the story. After you read each page, invite children to talk about the illustration.

▶ **What do the words on this page tell you about Clifford?**

▶ **Do the pictures help you understand what the girl means? How?**

▶ **How do you know Clifford is bigger than ordinary dogs?**

Help children see the humor of the story as shown in the pictures. Encourage children to share what they find funny about the story. Then discuss what is real and what is make-believe.

Clifford the Big Red Dog

Respond to the Literature

TALK ABOUT IT

Share Personal Responses Invite children to have a conversation about what it would be like to own a dog like Clifford.

▶ **Would you like to have a dog like Clifford? Why or why not?**

▶ **Why would having Clifford be different from having a regular-sized dog?**

▶ **What if Clifford came to your home? How could you keep him?**

THINK ABOUT IT

Following Rules When you have a dog, there are rules you have to follow to keep your dog from being a nuisance to people in your community.

▶ **Does Elizabeth seem to take good care of Clifford?**

▶ **If you have a pet, do you have rules that you have to follow?**

Invite children who have dogs to tell about some of the rules, such as keeping a dog on a leash. Then ask these questions:

▶ **Why would Clifford be a good dog to have in your community?**

▶ **What could you do so that Clifford could get along in your community?**

TECHNOLOGY

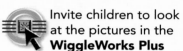

Invite children to look at the pictures in the **WiggleWorks Plus** selection, *Clifford the Big Red Dog* and to retell the book in their own words, using the Record and Playback tools. Encourage children to compare their retelling with Emily Elizabeth's story.

My Read and Write Book, p. 16

TECHNOLOGY

Record the following teacher message in the My Book Area: *Emily Elizabeth ends the book with a question for you. She says, "I'll keep Clifford . . . Wouldn't you?" Look through the book and then write your answer. Tell why you would or would not keep Clifford the big red dog. Then use the Paint tools to draw a picture of Clifford.*

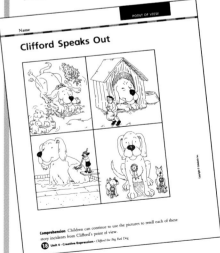

My Read and Write Book, pp. 17–18

Shared Writing

ADD A PAGE

Invite children to create a new page for *Clifford the Big Red Dog*.

- Working in small groups, have them think of another thing that Emily Elizabeth might say about her big red dog.
- Then help them write it in a sentence using the letters they know.
- Invite children to illustrate their page and share their work.

Repeated Reading

RECALLING AND SEQUENCING THE STORY

Reread the story *Clifford the Big Red Dog*. Before you read the text on each page, invite a volunteer to tell what's going to happen next. Encourage the student to use the picture clues to retell that part of the story. Then read the text to confirm the child's retelling.

READ AND WRITE INDEPENDENTLY

Journal Invite children to enjoy *Clifford the Big Red Dog* with a partner. They can take turns reading the text, using the pictures to remind themselves of the things that Emily Elizabeth says about Clifford. Invite children to draw and write in their Journals about a pet.

Comprehension Check

ACT IT OUT

Guide pairs of children to pretend to be Emily Elizabeth and Clifford. Keep the book handy so that children can look up situations to act out if they need to. Remind children to pretend that the person role-playing Clifford is very, very big! Give time for the partners to switch roles.

CENTER WORKSHOPS

Art

A Toy for Clifford

Dogs love to play, and dogs love toys. Invite children to draw pictures of toys that they think Clifford might enjoy. The challenge—and the reason you need large sheets of butcher paper—is that the pictures that they draw must be actual size! If Clifford had a ball to play with, how big would that have to be? How about a bone? Ask children to create an actual-size picture of a toy that they think Clifford would enjoy. Encourage children to add a caption to their picture.

Observation: Notice how children go about the task of deciding on a giant toy.

MATERIALS

- Crayons or markers
- Scissors
- Large sheets of butcher paper

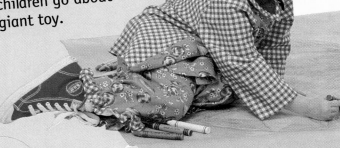

Math 123

How Big Is Clifford?

Let children look through magazines to cut out pictures of dogs. When they have a good collection of dogs, children can work together to arrange the pictures in order, from smallest to largest. Leave a lot of space after the picture of the largest dog, because that's where children can draw a picture of Clifford. Their picture of Clifford will show how much bigger they think Clifford is than the biggest dog.

Some children might want to find other ways to group the dogs, such as by color or type. Ask children to share their grouping method.

Observation: Notice how children order the pictures.

MATERIALS

- Magazines
- Mural paper
- Scissors
- Paste
- Red markers, black markers

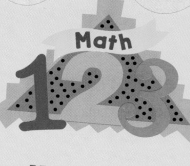

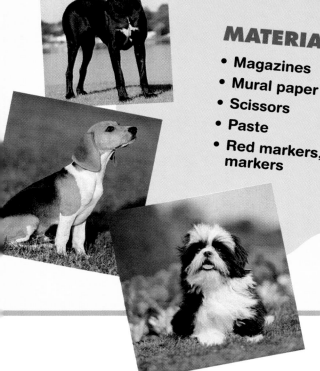

DAY 7 OBJECTIVES

CHILDREN WILL:

- listen for alliteration
- recognize consonant /p/p
- write letter *Pp*
- talk about the SourceCard
- create new verses to a song
- read High-Frequency Reader: *Can You See It?*
- engage in Center Workshops

MATERIALS

- *Creative Expression,* SourceCard 2
- *Alphabatics*
- ABC Card: *Pp*
- High-Frequency Reader: *Can You See It?*
- My Alphabet Book, p. 18

TECHNOLOGY

 Encourage children to use the drawing and writing tools in the **WiggleWorks Plus** Write area.

My Alphabet Book, p. 18

Read the SourceCard

 **DAILY PHONICS**

 *and Read the High-Frequency Reader*

Consonant /p/p

Ⓐ PHONOLOGICAL AWARENESS

Alliteration Write the following alliterative sentence on the chalkboard:

The purple penguin ate a pack of peanuts.

Read aloud the sentence and ask children what sound they hear at the beginning of *purple* and *penguin*. Then invite children to repeat the sentence and count the number of times they hear **/p/.**

Ⓑ CONNECT SOUND-SPELLING

Introduce Consonant /p/p Page through *Alphabatics* until you get to the *Pp* page. Point out that the letter *p* stands for **/p/** as in *plane*.

- Ask children to say the sound **/p/** with you. Have them exaggerate **/p/** as they say *plane.*

If available, show children the ABC Card for *Pp.* Have them say the name of the letter and the picture.

Letter Formation

WRITE THE LETTER

Write *Pp* on the chalkboard. Point out the capital and small forms of the letter. Repeat the rhyme below as you model how to form the letter.

- Have children write both forms of the letter in the air with their fingers. Ask children to make the letter's sound as they practice writing. Invite volunteers up to the chalkboard to practice writing the letters.

> Pp
>
> **Head straight down, but don't you roam.**
> *(Pull down straight.)*
> **Circle round and right back home.**
> *(Half-circle right, curve back to the line.)*

Share the SourceCard

Side One

SIDE ONE   **Telling a Story With Dance** Invite children to describe the pictures on the SourceCard.

▶ **Who do you think the people are? What movements are they making?**

Read the question "Do you like to dance?" and encourage children to answer it. Talk together about times children dance and the movements they make when they do dance.

Invite children to demonstrate favorite dance steps.

Side Two

SIDE TWO   **Expressing Feelings Through Movement** Point to the words of the song as you sing "If You're Happy" together. Encourage children to clap in appropriate places.

▶ **Have you ever been so happy that you wanted to sing? What made you feel that happy? What song did you feel like singing?**

▶ **How do you show that you are happy? How does your face look? How do you walk? Does everyone show they are happy in the same way?**

Shared Writing

CREATE NEW VERSES   What other actions could children perform as they sing "If You're Happy"? Ask children to suggest other feelings they could sing about. Help children write new verses to the song, using the song's format.

> If you're silly and you know it.
>   Go "hee-hee!"

Sing the new verses together, making the sounds and movements children suggest.

ESL/ELD

▲ Elicit words for other feelings and write them on the board. You may use words like *silly, sad,* or *jolly.* Then elicit body actions that could go along with the meaning of each word. For example, you may snap your fingers or make a frown. Once you have written a few words on the chalkboard, add them to the song. **(PANTOMIME)**

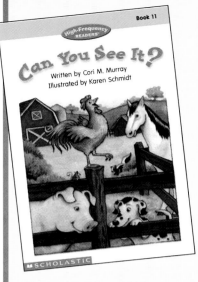

Book 11

Can You See It?

Revisit High-Frequency Reader

REREAD THE BOOK

Invite children to join you as you read *Can You See It?* again. Have children read the four words in the first sentence that they have already learned. (*can, you, see, it*) Review these words. Repeat with the next sentence. (*I, see,* and *a*)

DECODING STRATEGIES

As you go through the book, point to each word, the picture clue, and any other sound-spellings the children have learned, pausing long enough for children to read before you do. Model blending words. For example, have children use their knowledge of **/m/m** to decode *mouse*.

Think Aloud *At the beginning of the word, I see the letter* m. *I know that* m *stands for* **/m/**. *In the picture I see a mouse. The word* mouse *begins with* **/m/**. *This word is* mouse. *That makes sense.*

CONCEPTS OF PRINT: END PUNCTUATION

Display the sentence strip for page one. Read it and review the punctuation mark that ends each sentence. Cover the end punctuation mark in each pair of sentences. Have children decide which sentences need a period and which need a question mark.

Can you see it?	**I see a rooster.**
Can you see it?	**I see a pig.**

ORAL LANGUAGE: FARM ANIMALS

Point out that the story takes place on a farm. Have children name the farm animal on each page. Then ask them to name other farm animals.

READ FOR FLUENCY

Give each child their own copy of *Can You See It?*

• Invite children to read their books with a partner, one child reading the question and the other the answer. They can both pretend to be the animal named.

READ AND WRITE INDEPENDENTLY

Journal Have children read *Can You See It?* on their own. Children can write about their favorite farm animals in their Journals.

HOME/SCHOOL CONNECTION

Children can take home their High-Frequency Reader and work with family members on a new book about pets.

CENTER WORKSHOPS

Music & Movement

Weather Dances

Many cultures have dances, like rain dances, that have been created to bring on a certain kind of weather considered important for daily activities.

- Let partners look through the weather pictures to decide what kind of weather dance they would like to create.
- Guide partners to think about how they would act in the kind of weather they have chosen.
- Partners can take turns in the roles of drummer and dancer as they perform their weather dance. The rest of the class guesses what kind of weather the dance is for.

Observation: How do children use movement to express their ideas?

MATERIALS

- Percussion instruments
- Pictures that show different kinds of weather

Social Studies

A Collage of Feelings

Children can make a collage of magazine cutouts showing different emotions.

- Divide a piece of poster board into three sections. Label the sections "Mad," "Sad," and "Glad."
- Invite children to cut out pictures of people or animals expressing their feelings through action, body language, and facial expression.
- Children can sort the pictures by emotion and can glue them on the appropriate section of the poster.

Observation: How do children verbalize the connection between movements and emotions?

MATERIALS

- Poster board
- Old magazines
- Scissors
- Glue

CHILDREN WILL:

- orally blend word parts
- blend words with phonogram *-op*
- read and respond to *Mama Zooms*
- make inferences
- write a story extension
- join in on patterned text
- engage in Center Workshops

MATERIALS

- *Mama Zooms*
- *My Read and Write Book,* p. 19

 The Big Book is available on audiocassette in the Literacy Place Listening Center.

Share the Read Aloud

DAILY PHONICS

Consonant /p/p

A PHONOLOGICAL AWARENESS

Oral Blending Say aloud the following word parts. Ask children to blend them. Provide corrective feedback.

/p/ . . . ig	/p/. . . an	/p/ . . . ull
ho . . . /p/	ma . . . /p/	ti . . . /p/

B CONNECT SOUND-SPELLING

Introduce the Phonogram *-op* Write the phonogram *-op* on the board. Say the sounds that *-op* stands for. Point out that *-op* ends in /p/.

Add the letter *m* to the beginning of *-op* and blend the sounds to form the word *mop*.

Think Aloud *I can put the letters* m *and* op *together to make the word* mop. *Let's say the word slowly as I move my finger under the letters. Listen to how I string together the sounds to make the word: mmmooop, mmoop, mop.*

Blend List the following words and sentences on the chalkboard. Have volunteers read each word and sentence aloud. Model blending where necessary.

- **hop**
- **pop**
- **mop**
- **I can hop.**

Build Background

ORAL LANGUAGE: PRETENDING

Ask children to talk about the things they pretend to do.

▶ **Do you ever pretend to gallop on a horse, fly an airplane, or drive a car? How else do you pretend?**

Talk about the meaning of the word *zooms*.

PREVIEW AND PREDICT

Read the title and the author/illustrator's name. Ask children to look at the picture on the cover and share what they think the boy and his mother are doing. Let children preview some of the pictures in the book.

Share the Read Aloud

MAKE INFERENCES

Read the story aloud. As you read, ask children what the pictures reveal about the meaning of the title, *Mama Zooms*.

When children start to see the relationship between the art and the text, guide them to make inferences about the story.

▶ **What is the zooming machine?**

Mama Zooms

Respond to the Literature

TALK ABOUT IT

Share Personal Experiences Encourage children to talk about their reactions to the story.

▶ **Are the boy and his mother having fun together? How can you tell?**

▶ **What was the "zooming machine?" Were you surprised to find out that it was the mother's wheelchair?**

▶ **What is the story mainly about?**

THINK ABOUT IT

Movement and Sound Talk together about what the boy and his mother pretended. Review the book illustrations and talk about the movements that the boy and his mother are making.

▶ **What movement is the boy making as he pretends to be riding a racehorse? What movement is he making as he pretends to drive a race car? What is he pretending to hold?**

Talk about the sounds the boy and his mother might make as they pretend different things. Encourage children to have fun demonstrating these sounds and acting out the movements.

MODIFY Instruction

ESL/ELD

▲ As you read the story aloud, encourage English language learners to follow along by "reading" the illustrations. During the follow-up discussion, point to the pictures to prompt children to retell the story. **(RETELL)**

MODIFY Instruction

ESL/ELD

▲ Use the book illustrations to spark children's interest and to reinforce their understanding of the text. For further practice, tape the story for children and have them listen to the audiotape with a fluent classmate. **(AUDIO CLUES)**

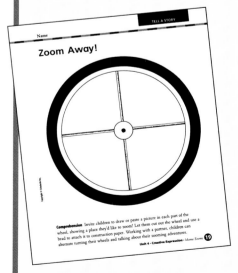

Zoom Away!

My Read and Write Book, p. 19

Shared Writing

FINISH THE SENTENCE

Write the following sentence on a chart:

"Mama zooms me through a puddle and she's my _____."

Read the sentence with children, and ask them to suggest words to end it. Invite children to write their suggestions on the chart, writing the letters that stand for the sounds they know.

Mama zooms me through a puddle and she's my.... ship at sea.

Show children the sentence in the book, and read it together. Ask volunteers to finish the sentence by writing the words "ship at sea."

Invite children to add illustrations for all their suggestions.

Repeated Reading

JOIN IN

Reread the story, encouraging children to join in on all the lines that begin "and she's my. . . ." Remind them that the boy's clothing will help them figure out the words at the end of the line. Pause long enough so children have a chance to read the words before you do.

READ AND WRITE INDEPENDENTLY

Journal Place *Mama Zooms* in the Reading Center so that children can enjoy it on their own or in small groups. Children can write or draw in their Journals about something else that the boy and his mother pretend to be.

☑ Comprehension Check

ACT IT OUT

As you read the story aloud, encourage children to act out each adventure the boy in the story imagines. Invite them to make movements and sounds as they pretend. For example, when the story says, "Mama zooms me across the lawn," children can pretend to ride a racehorse and make galloping sounds.

CENTER WORKSHOPS

Science

MATERIALS

- Toy cars
- Boards
- Blocks

Zooming

Ask children how they can make toy cars zoom. Encourage children to use blocks and boards to make ramps and inclines, exploring their effect on the speed of the toy cars.

Ask children if the cars zoom when they move them on the flat floor. Do the cars zoom when they go down the ramp? What happens when children make their ramps steeper?

Observation: How do children make ramps and inclines? What changes do they notice in the speed of the toy cars?

Art

MATERIALS

- Paper
- Markers or crayons
- Paints

Our Imagination Book

Talk together about all the different things children pretend.

- Encourage children to draw or paint pictures of something they like to pretend, places they pretend to go, or people they pretend to be. Ask children to label their pictures with their names and comments.

- Staple the pictures together, and write "Our Imaginations" on the cover. List children as the authors and illustrators.

- Read the book together and congratulate children on their creativity.

Observation: What pictures do children draw and how do they describe them?

DAY 9 OBJECTIVES

CHILDREN WILL:

- generate rhyming words
- recognize sound-spelling relationship for /p/p
- connect spoken words to written words
- review high-frequency words
- read My Book: *My Name Is Sam*
- engage in Center Workshops

MATERIALS

- *Big Book of Rhymes and Rhythms,* p. 21
- Sentence Strips for "Pease Porridge"
- ABC Card: *Pp*
- *Mama Zooms*
- My Book: *My Name Is Sam*
- My Read and Write Book, p. 20

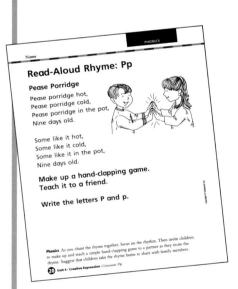

My Read and Write Book, p. 20

For additional practice see *Scholastic Phonics K,* pp. 83–86. See also Sound and Letter Book: *Seven Pigs.*

Sounds and Letters

 DAILY PHONICS  and Read My Book

Consonant /p/p

A PHONOLOGICAL AWARENESS

Rhyme Read aloud the rhyme "Pease Porridge" from the *Big Book of Rhymes and Rhythms.* Ask children what sound they hear at the beginning of the words *Pease* and *porridge.* Invite children to repeat the words as you exaggerate the beginning sound.

Have children say the rhyme with you. Help them think of other words that rhyme with *hot* and *cold.*

Big Book of Rhymes and Rhythms, p. 21

B CONCEPTS OF PRINT

Place the *Big Book of Rhymes and Rhythms,* the Sentence Strips for "Pease Porridge," and a pocket chart in the Reading Center. Then do the following:

- Read "Pease Porridge," asking children to clap in time with the rhythm. Then reread the rhyme together. Ask volunteers to place the appropriate Sentence Strip in a pocket chart as you read each line.
- Invite children to frame each word in a sentence with their fingers.
- Then have children point to all of the words that begin with *Pp.*

Pease porridge hot,

Pease porridge cold,

Pease porridge in the pot,

Nine days old.

MODIFY Instruction

EXTRA HELP

■ Children might enjoy forming the letter *Pp* in trays of sand or cornmeal. As children form the letter, provide auditory and contextual reinforcement by making the sound and saying words that begin with *Pp.* Invite children to repeat the sound and words after you. **(HANDS-ON-LEARNING)**

C CONNECT SOUND-SPELLING

Alphabetic Principle Display an ABC card for the letter *p*. Review that the letter *p* stands for the sound children hear at the beginning of *pencil*. Then invite children to look through the pages of *Mama Zooms* and point to the words that begin with *Pp*. (*puts, puddle, push*) Read each word aloud as it is identified, emphasizing the **/p/** sound.

ABC Book Explain to children that they are going to make a new page for their own ABC Book. Have children suggest animals, objects, and people whose names begin with **/p/**. Invite children to work together to create the *Pp* page for their ABC Books.

Hop on Top Write the word *hop* at the top of a word ladder. Ask children to change the first letter to make a new word. Suggest the letters: *p, m, f, t,* and *d*. Help them blend the sounds. Invite children to hop in place if they make a real word.

D VOCABULARY: HIGH-FREQUENCY WORDS

On the chalkboard write the following sentence: *I can see it.* Review each word with children using the read-spell-write routine.

Write each word on a word card. Pick one and help children figure out the word by giving clues such as:

• It starts like *cat. (can)*

• It has only one letter. *(I)*

• It has two letters exactly the same. *(see)*

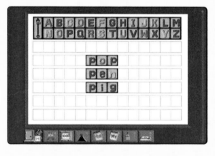

TECHNOLOGY

 Write the words *pop, pen,* and *pig* on the **WiggleWorks Plus** Magnet Board and help children read them. Explode the words to mix up the letters. Then invite children to rewrite the words.

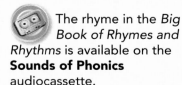 The rhyme in the *Big Book of Rhymes and Rhythms* is available on the **Sounds of Phonics** audiocassette.

My Name Is Sam

GIFTED & TALENTED

✳ Invite children to use their knowledge of the high-frequency words *my*, *I*, and *can* and the sound-spellings they have learned to create a book about themselves. Have them model their pages on *My Name Is Sam*. (BUILD ON SUCCESS)

Read My Book

INTRODUCE THE BOOK

Let children know that they are going to get their own book that they can read on their own and take home.

▶ **How would you describe yourself to someone you are just meeting?**

PREVIEW AND PREDICT

Pass out copies of *My Name Is Sam*. Read the title and the author's and illustrator's names.

▶ **What do you notice on the cover?**

▶ **Who do you think the book might be about?**

READ TOGETHER

Read the My Book with children, tracking the print as you read. Guide children to read along in their copies and to look for the things Sam can do. At the appropriate point in the text, children can write their name and something they like to do. Invite them to draw their own illustration to go with their words.

PHONICS

Ask children to say the word *name* aloud.

▶ **What letter stands for the sound you hear at the beginning of the word?**

Encourage children to use other sound-spellings they know to help read new words.

READ AND WRITE INDEPENDENTLY

Journal Encourage children to read *My Name Is Sam* on their own or in small groups. Provide crayons and invite children to color the illustrations.

HOME/SCHOOL CONNECTION

Children can take home their My Book to share with family members and friends. Suggest that children work with a family member to write a book about the sounds and movements they like to make.

CENTER WORKSHOPS

Music & Movement

MATERIALS

- **Big Book of Rhymes and Rhythms**

Calling All Songwriters

Open the book to "Polly, Put the Kettle On." Sing the familiar melody to the children, and then invite them to sing along. Ask children which name in the song begins with **Pp**.

Let volunteers substitute other names they know that begin with **Pp**. (Let them interview another class for name ideas.) Encourage them to make a list of the names. Tape-record children chanting the rhyme in unison.

Observation: Listen to children's ideas for **Pp** names. Are they hearing the sound of /p/?

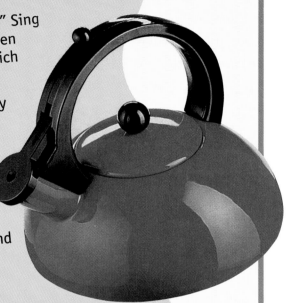

Cooking

MATERIALS

- **Popped popcorn or popper and unpopped popcorn**
- **ABC Card: Pp**

Pp's Are Popping!

Pop corn with the class or bring in already-popped corn. Talk about the sounds and movement of the kernels as they pop.

Children can pretend that they are popcorn kernels by scrunching down on the floor. As you describe the heat getting hotter and hotter, encourage them to use their bodies to get bigger and bigger and to finally pop up to become pieces of popcorn.

Provide the ABC Card **Pp** as a model and let each child take some popcorn and use the pieces to form **Pp**. Then they can eat their letters!

Observation: Watch how children form the letter **Pp**.

CHILDREN WILL:

- sing a song
- compare and contrast the books they have shared
- participate in writing a group chart
- differentiate sound positions
- consonant review
- create a final project

MATERIALS

- *Mama Zooms*
- *The Three Little Pigs*
- *Clifford the Big Red Dog*
- *The Itsy Bitsy Spider*
- Picture Cards, R33–34

TECHNOLOGY

Encourage students to use the drawing and writing tools in the **WiggleWorks Plus** Write area to complete the project and activities.

Put It All Together

Sum It Up

RECALL SOUNDS AND MOVEMENTS

Remind children that they have been reading and talking about ways that stories can be told with movement and sounds. Encourage them to recall the stories you have read together. Write the titles of the books they remember on chart paper.

ORAL LANGUAGE: SONG

Invite children to sing and act out the traditional song "Hokey Pokey." Place yarn on their right wrists so they know which hand is the right one.

Hokey Pokey

**You put your right hand in,
You put your right hand out,
You put your right hand in,
And you shake it all about.
You do the Hokey Pokey,
And you turn yourself around,
That's what it's all about.**

Language Experience Chart

COMPARE AND CONTRAST CHART

Display the books that children have read during the previous nine sessions. Encourage children to talk about the stories and the sounds and movements in each. Answer any questions they may have about the books.

Make a language chart labeled "We Tell Stories With Movements and Sound." Talk about how the author of each story used movements and/or sound to tell the story. Write children's responses on the language chart. It might look like the one shown.

We Tell Stories With Movements and Sound

Mama Zooms	The Three Little Pigs	The Itsy Bitsy Spider	Clifford the Big Red Dog
A boy and his mother pretend to zoom to many places in her wheelchair.	The wolf keeps trying to huff and puff and blow the pigs' houses down.	We used hand and body movements to show what happened in parts of the verses.	The pictures show Clifford moving around, doing things normal-sized dogs do.

Observation:

How are children doing? Are they:
- sharing information about stories they've read?
- recognizing how the stories relate to the theme?
- easily recalling story details?
- using story language in their conversations?

TEACHER TIP

Many languages have only a few consonant sounds that can appear at the end of words. In Spanish, only /s/, /t/, /l/, /r/, and /d/ appear in the final position. In Mandarin, only /n/ and /ng/ appear in this position, and in Hmong only /ng/ exists. In Laotian, most words end in a vowel sound. Therefore, children speaking these languages might need support with ending sound activities.

DAILY PHONICS

Maintenance

Ⓐ PHONOLOGICAL AWARENESS

Beginning or End? Show children the following picture cards: cup, pig, mop, top, pan, pen, lip. Have them pat their heads if the word begins with /p/ as in *pat*. Have them hop if the word ends with /p/ as in *hop*.

Ⓑ PHONICS MAINTENANCE

Simon Says Have each child make letter cards for *p* and *l*. Then invite them to play a game of Simon Says. Say the following words: *pan, leg, like, pig, paste, laugh, penguin, lake, pot*.

Have children segment the beginning sound and then hold up the card with the letter that stands for that sound. Invite them to take a step forward when they hold up the correct letter card.

You may want to continue with other pairs of letters such as *k* and *m* or *l* and *f*.

WEEKS 3 AND 4
PROJECT

Create, Plan, and Perform

During the third and fourth weeks, children have explored different ways that sound and movement can be used to tell stories. For the final project, children can create new endings for *The Three Little Pigs* and can use sound and movement to dramatize the new story endings.

Talk with children about the ending of *The Three Little Pigs*. Ask children to think of other ways that the story might have ended. Write children's ideas on chart paper.

MATERIALS

- **Chart paper**
- **Marker**
- **Instruments**
- **Art materials**

BENCHMARKS

Monitor children's progress. Are they:

- participating in creating movements?
- demonstrating listening skills?
- creating alternative endings?
- dramatizing new story endings?

Guide children to form small groups. Read aloud children's suggested endings to the story, and invite each group to select one ending to dramatize.

Work with each group to help children act out their new story ending.

▶ **What movements would the characters make?**

▶ **What sounds might they make or hear?**

Children can practice making different movements.

Help them think of ways to make different sounds using instruments, their voices, or objects. Encourage children to create props to use in their performance—children might enjoy making masks out of paper plates, for example. Let each group rehearse its performance.

When everyone is ready, invite each group to act out its new ending to the story for the rest of the class.

Talk together about all of the sounds and movements children used to act out their story endings. Congratulate everyone on their hard work and creativity.

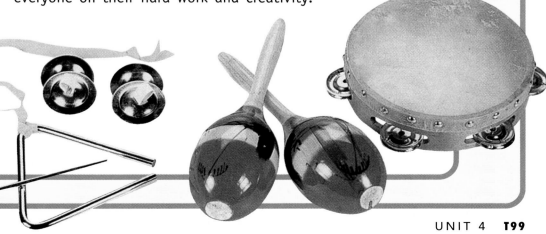

WEEKS
5 AND 6

Kindergarten Goals
for Weeks 5 and 6

Oral Language/ Vocabulary

- participating in rhymes, songs, conversations, and discussions
- participating in choral reading
- discussing shape words, school words, and names of fruits
- exploring story vocabulary

Reading

- building alphabetic knowledge
- participating in shared reading
- engaging in emergent reading
- exploring concepts of print
- sequencing story events
- investigating picture clues and story patterns
- recognizing setting
- reading high-frequency words

Writing

- creating shape stories
- extending the story
- writing letters: *Qq, Rr*
- writing steps in a process
- writing stories about pictures
- writing sentences about shadows
- engaging in shared writing
- writing independently in Journals

Listening/Speaking/ Viewing

- listening responsively to stories and other texts read aloud
- identifying rhyme
- developing phonological awareness
- retelling a story in their own words
- presenting dramatic interpretations of stories
- contributing to group discussions
- relating personal experiences to literature
- comparing stories
- demonstrating visual literacy

Daily Phonics: *Qq* and *Rr*

- reciting classic poems, songs, and nursery rhymes
- naming and recognizing the letters
- recognizing sound/letter relationships
- generating words with /kw/, /r/
- decoding words using /kw/*qu,* /r/*r*

Center Workshops and Project

- acquiring world knowledge through cross-curricular activities
- creating a Meet the Authors Celebration

WEEKS 5 AND 6
RESOURCES

Big Book
Meet the Author/Illustrator

Pat Hutchins grew up in Yorkshire, England. She loved drawing as a child and always knew that she wanted to be an artist. Today she lives in London with her husband and two sons.

Available as audiocassette

Big Book of Rhymes and Rhythms

For teaching phonological awareness, the alphabet, and concepts of print.

- "*Q* Was a Quail"
- "Ride a Cock-Horse"

Available as audiocassette

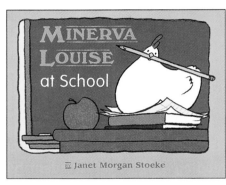

Read Aloud
Meet the Author/Illustrator

Before she wrote and illustrated children's books, Janet Morgan Stoeke had many different jobs. She worked in a bookstore, was a gymnastics instructor, a waitress, a museum docent, and an advertising designer. When *Minerva Louise* won first prize in a picture book contest, it marked the beginning of a new career.

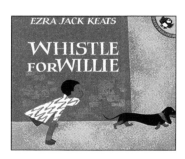

Read Aloud
Meet the Author/Illustrator

Ezra Jack Keats believed that good pictures told their own stories, so when he finished a set of illustrations, he would put them on the wall. If the characters seemed to be talking to him, he knew that they were right.

ABC Book
Meet the Author/Illustrator

Alphabatics was Suse MacDonald's first book. By manipulating the position of each letter, Suse MacDonald believes she brings the alphabet "into the child's world of action and visual image."

Side One

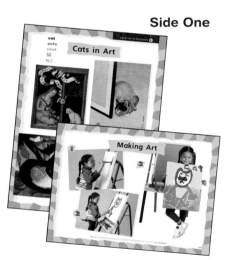

Side Two

SourceCard
- Cats in Art
- Making Art

High-Frequency Reader

My Read and Write Book

My Books

To take home to share.

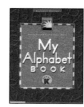

My Alphabet Book

ESL/ELD Teaching Guide

Storytelling

"The Spider Weaver"

a folk tale from Japan

Introducing the Mentor

Pat Mora loves to tell stories. Although her own children are grown, neighborhood children often read and tell stories with her.

DAYS AT A GLANCE

WEEKS 5 AND 6

	Daily Phonics	Literature	Shared Writing	Workshops and Projects
DAY 1	Phonological Awareness: Auditory Discrimination Review /n/n, /o/o, /p/p	*Alphabatics* by Suse MacDonald *ABC BOOK*	Create Shape Stories	Games: It's a Match Writing: Class ABC Book
DAY 2	**Consonant /kw/qu** Phonological Awareness: Oral Segmentation: Beginning Sounds	*Good-Night, Owl!* by Pat Hutchins *BIG BOOK · LITTLE BOOK*	Extend the Story	Science: For the Birds Listening: Listen to the Birds
DAY 3	**Consonant /kw/qu** Phonological Awareness: Alliteration Introduce Sound-Spelling	*Good-Night, Owl!* by Pat Hutchins *BIG BOOK · LITTLE BOOK* **High-Frequency Reader:** *We Like Fruit*	Concepts of Print: Match Speech to Written Word Write *Qq* Make a Class Book	Art: Owl's Tree Math: How Many Animals?
DAY 4	**Consonant /kw/qu** Phonological Awareness: Oral Blending Review Sound-Spelling	*Minerva Louise at School* by Janet Morgan Stoeke *READ ALOUD*	Extend the Story	Art: Create a Character Games: How Many Ways Can You Use It?
DAY 5	**Consonant /kw/qu** Phonological Awareness: Rhyme Maintain Sound-Spelling	*"Q Was a Quail"* a rhyme *Alphabatics* **My Book:** *I Can Draw*	Concepts of Print: Uppercase and Lowercase Letters High-Frequency Word: *and*	Health & Fitness: *Qq* Moves Alphabet: *Qq* with Quills

	Daily Phonics	Literature	Shared Writing	Workshops and Projects
DAY 6	**Consonant /r/r** Phonological Awareness: Rhyme	*The Spider Weaver* retold by Florence Sakade	Write Steps in a Process	Art: Weaving Cloud Pictures
DAY 7	**Consonant /r/r** Phonological Awareness: Alliteration Introduce Sound-Spelling	**SourceCard** Cats in Art Making Art **High-Frequency Reader:** *We Like Fruit*	Write Stories About Pictures Write *Rr*	Art: Mixed Media Games: Sort the Steps
DAY 8	**Consonant /r/r** Phonological Awareness: Oral Blending Review Sound-Spelling Phonogram -an	*Whistle for Willie* by Ezra Jack Keats READ ALOUD	Write Shadow Sentences	Art: Make a Picture With Collage Materials Dramatic Play: A Box is . . .
DAY 9	**Consonant /r/r** Phonological Awareness: Rhyme Maintain Sound-Spelling	**"Ride a Cock-Horse"** a nursery rhyme *Good-Night, Owl!* **My Book:** *We Like to Build*	Concepts of Print: Connect Spoken and Written Words High-Frequency Words	Science: Rocks, Rivers, and Rainbows Math: Rock Hound
DAY 10	Phonological Awareness: Auditory Discrimination Phonics Maintenance	**Review Books from Weeks 5 and 6**	Make a Compare and Contrast Chart	Project: Meet the Authors Celebration

Share the ABC Book

DAY 1 OBJECTIVES

DAY 1 OBJECTIVES

CHILDREN WILL:

- identify words with the same beginning sounds
- review consonants /n/n, /p/p, and vowel /o/o
- read and respond to *Alphabatics*
- recognize *Qq* and *Rr*
- create shape stories
- engage in Center Workshops

MATERIALS

- *Alphabatics*

GUIDED READING

To conclude each day's reading session, meet with guided reading groups. You might use Scholastic's Guided Reading Library or other books in your library.

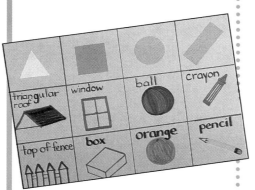

Warm-Up: Wordplay

Ⓐ PHONOLOGICAL AWARENESS

Nina Likes . . . Invite children to play a game of "Nina likes . . ." Name some objects. If an object's name begins with **/n/** as in *Nina*, children should say that it is something that Nina likes. Use the following words: *nickels, cars, nests, bacon, notes, noodles, mops*. Play additional rounds using "Ollie likes . . ." and "Pablo likes . . ." to review the sounds of **/o/** and **/p/**.

Ⓑ PHONICS MAINTENANCE

Review Letters /n/n, /o/o, /p/p Have children chant the alphabet as you page through *Alphabatics*. Stop on the pages for *Nn, Oo,* and *Pp*. Have children name the letter and the object pictured on each card. Encourage them to name another object that begins with each sound.

Build Background

ORAL LANGUAGE: SHAPES

Point out objects in the classroom that have familiar shapes such as triangles, squares, circles, and rectangles. After looking at each shape ask children:

▶ **Have you seen anything else with the same shape?**

Make a chart with the different shapes pictured at the top. List the objects children name under each shape. Afterwards, invite children to draw a picture of one of the objects and add it to the chart.

PREVIEW AND PREDICT

Display the cover of *Alphabatics*. Review the title and author/illustrator's name.

▶ **Do you notice any shapes on the cover? What funny things has the author/illustrator done to the letters?**

Alphabatics

Read the ABC Book

ALPHABETIC KNOWLEDGE: *Qq* AND *Rr*

Open *Alphabatics* and show children the first page. Review how the letter becomes part of the picture on the next page.

- Read the word on the first page and point out that this word begins with the letter *Aa*.

- As you read, invite children to notice the uppercase and lowercase letters. Have them tell you which version of the letter the artist used to make the picture.

- Stop at the pages for *Qq* or *Rr*. Have children notice the letters. Say the names of the pictures and have children note the beginning sounds.

Respond to the Literature

TALK ABOUT IT

Share Personal Responses Talk with children about the ABC book.

▶ **How do you think the author/illustrator decided what to include on each page?**

▶ **Did this book give you ideas about different things that letters can become? What could the letter that begins your name become?**

THINK ABOUT IT

Focus on *Qq* and *Rr* Return to the pages for *Qq* and *Rr*. Have children say the letter names and point to the uppercase and lowercase forms. Review the sound by saying the name of the pictures. Invite children to answer riddles about words that begin with one of these two letters.

▶ (Draw a question mark on the board.) **This mark follows a ...** *(question)*

▶ **This is a woman who wears a crown.** *(queen)*

▶ **This animal is like a mouse. Its name rhymes with *hat*.** *(rat)*

▶ **This is what you do on a bike or in a car.** *(ride)*

Write each new word on the board. Have children underline the letters *Qq* and *Rr*.

EXTRA HELP

■ Some children may have difficulty visualizing how each letter can be formed into an object. Provide magnetic letters or other letter manipulatives for children to handle. Encourage them to turn the letters in different positions to stimulate ideas about what objects the letters look like. **(HANDS-ON LEARNING)**

ESL/ELD

▲ Provide a variety of pictures cut out from magazines. Invite children to study the pictures to find different shapes as well as shapes that could form the letters they know. Have children use magnetic letters or other manipulatives as stimulus. **(USE VISUALS)**

Shared Writing

CREATE SHAPE STORIES

Have children draw a circle and invite them to turn it into a drawing of something they have seen. Model some examples by suggesting that a sun and a ball are shaped like a circle.

Then encourage children to write a label for the drawing that says: *A circle is a* _____ .

Continue the activity by substituting other familiar shapes. Invite children to share their favorite shape story with the rest of the class.

LABEL SHAPES

Invite children to write the shape name of various classroom objects on sticky notes. Then ask them to label those items. Children can use the Shapes chart to help them write their notes.

Repeated Reading

RETELL PICTURE STORIES

Reread the ABC book with children. As you read, pause and invite children to point out places in pictures where they see the shape of the letters. Have them tell the story of what is happening to each letter in the pictures.

READ AND WRITE INDEPENDENTLY

Journal Invite children to reread *Alphabatics* on their own or in small groups. Children can write or draw in their Journals about their favorite letter page.

☑ Comprehension Check

ACT IT OUT

Have children work in small groups to use their bodies to form a letter. After children create a letter ask them what shapes they had to make with their bodies.

CENTER WORKSHOPS

Games

It's a Match!

Children can make an animal/letter memory game.

Invite children to draw an animal for each letter of the alphabet on individual index cards. Suggest that they use the Animal Sorting Cards and the alphabet books that they have studied as resources.

Children can turn both the ABC Cards and the index cards they make face down. Then they can take turns turning two cards over as they search for letter/animal matches.

Observation: What strategies do children use as they play the memory game?

MATERIALS

- ABC Cards
- Index Cards
- Crayons or markers
- Animal Sorting Cards
- *Alphabatics; A Was Once an Apple Pie; Apples, Alligators and also Alphabets*

Writing

Class ABC Book

On a chart, work with children to list shapes and objects that begin with the letters *Aa* to *Zz*. Let each child choose one thing from the list to illustrate.

Label each picture with the name of the object and the first letter of the object's name.

When children have made pictures for every letter, work together to put the pictures in the correct order. Staple the pages together, including a cover. Children can think of a title for their class ABC book and can list themselves as illustrators.

Place the book in the Reading Center.

Observation: How well do children make letter and word correspondences?

MATERIALS

- Paper
- Crayons
- Markers
- Collage materials

DAY 2 OBJECTIVES

CHILDREN WILL:

- orally segment words
- recognize /kw/qu
- read and respond to *Good-Night, Owl!*
- recognize story patterns
- write a story extension
- engage in Center Workshops

MATERIALS

- *Good-Night, Owl!*

The Big Book is available on audiocassette in the Literacy Place Listening Center.

The song is available on the **Sounds of Phonics** audiocassette.

Share the Big Book

Consonant /kw/qu

PHONOLOGICAL AWARENESS

Oral Segmentation: Beginning Sounds Read the title of the song, "Six Little Ducks." Ask children what sound a duck makes. *(quack)*

- Say the word *quack,* isolating the beginning sounds: *qu-qu-quack.* Have children repeat.
- Sing or play "Six Little Ducks." Invite children to sing along starting with the second verse.
- Have children clap when they hear the word *quack.*

Six Little Ducks

Six little ducks that I once knew
Fat ones, skinny ones, fair ones too.
But the one little duck with the feather on his back
He led the others with a quack, quack, quack, quack, quack, quack.
He led the others with a quack, quack, quack.

2. Five little ducks that I once knew...

Build Background

ORAL LANGUAGE: OWLS

Discuss that a duck is a kind of bird. Then invite children to share what they know about another bird—the owl.

▶ **Where do owls live? When do they sleep?**

▶ **What sound do owls make?**

Discuss that owls sleep during the day and are awake all night.

PREVIEW AND PREDICT

Display *Good-Night, Owl!* Read the title and the name of the author/illustrator, tracking the print.

▶ **What animals do you see in the tree on the cover?**

Read the Big Book

As you read the story, encourage children to look closely at the illustrations and see if they can spot what has been added to each page. As children become familiar with the pattern of the story, encourage them to chime in with the repeated line, "and Owl tried to sleep." On the page that presents the cumulative list of all the creatures that kept Owl awake, let children echo the sounds after you've read them.

Good-Night, Owl!

Respond to the Literature

**TALK
ABOUT IT**

Share Personal Responses Encourage children to share their surprises and questions about the book.

▶ **What did you like best about this book? Did any part of it surprise you?**

▶ **What problem did Owl have? How did he solve it?**

▶ **How is this book like** *Listen to the Desert?* **How is it different?**

▶ **What sounds do you hear at night when you fall asleep?**

**THINK
ABOUT IT**

Sequence Animals Remind children that all of the creatures who arrive in the tree sleep at night and are awake during the day. Then look back into the book and ask children to name the creatures that arrived in the tree.

▶ **Who woke up Owl first as he tried to sleep?**

▶ **Who woke up Owl next?**

Write the animals children name on a chart and invite children to share in the writing. Encourage them to decorate the chart with drawings of each creature.

Noisy Creatures	
bees	crows
squirrel	woodpecker
starlings	cuckoo
jays	sparrows
robin	doves

ESL/ELD

▲ Reinforce awareness of sound-symbol relationships for English language learners. Prepare a matching game with pictures of the animals found in the story *Good-Night, Owl!* and another set of cards with the sounds they make. Have children work with an English-speaking partner to match the sound card with the animal. Ask the pair to explain why the two cards go together. **(WORK IN PAIRS)**

OBSERVATION

How are children doing?
Are they:

- using picture clues?
- recognizing story pattern?
- enjoying humor and surprise?
- using the language and sounds in the story during retellings?

Keep your observations in mind when planning Day 3, Revisit the Big Book.

PROFESSIONAL DEVELOPMENT

ADRIA KLEIN

Choral and Echo Reading

Choral and echo reading give children a chance to develop fluency. As they use more expression in repeated readings of stories, poems, and songs, children will be more confident and fluent.

Shared Writing

EXTEND THE STORY

Invite children to suggest another bird or animal that could visit Owl's tree and keep poor Owl awake. Then work together, following the pattern of the story, to write about Owl's new visitor. Have children help by writing the letters that they know. Remind children to write from left to right and from top to bottom.

> The tree toad croaked
> ribbit, ribbit
> and Owl tried to sleep.

Repeated Reading

CHORAL READING

When you reread the story, read the parts that tell what the night sleepers did, and let children read the sentences that tell about Owl. Children can read "Owl tried to sleep" whenever it appears. They can also read the surprise lines at the end. Tape-record the reading for children to share.

READ AND WRITE INDEPENDENTLY

Journal Put copies of *Good-Night, Owl!* and the audiocassette in the Reading Center so that children can enjoy it on their own or with a partner.

Suggest that children draw pictures in their Journals of their favorite story animal. Next to the pictures, they might write the animal's name and the sound it makes.

☑ Comprehension Check

ACT IT OUT

As you reread the story, let children imitate each of the creatures that kept Owl awake. They might hover and buzz like bees, hold nuts in their front paws and crunch like squirrels, and flap their wings and caw like crows. Invite some children to be Owl trying to sleep and making screeching sounds.

CENTER WORKSHOPS

Science

MATERIALS

- **Empty milk jugs**
- **Pine cones or cardboard tubes, twigs, empty grapefruit or coconut half**
- **String or wire**
- **Peanut butter, birdseed**

For the Birds

Children may enjoy making bird feeders that can be hung from a tree or stuck in the ground. Continue to feed the birds all year.

1. Roll a pine cone or a cardboard tube (to which you have already attached a string or wire) in peanut butter and then in birdseed.
2. Roll twigs in peanut butter and then in seed.
3. Fill an empty grapefruit or coconut half (to which you have attached a string or wire) with seed.
4. Cut an opening in a large milk jug. Attach a string or wire and fill the jug with seed.

Encourage children to observe how the birds use the feeders and to record their observations in their Journals.

Observation: Listen to children's predictions about what will happen to the feeders outside.

Listening

MATERIALS

- **Audubon audiotape of bird calls (available in public libraries)**
- **Audubon or Peterson Guide**
- **Tape recorder**
- **Blank audiotape**
- **Bird watcher or ornithologist**

Listen to the Birds

Help children locate pictures of the story birds in the bird guides and flag them with sticky notes. Listen together to the calls made by each of the birds on the tape.

- If possible tape-record each bird's call so that you have a tape recording that contains only the birds in *Good-Night, Owl!*
- Then children can listen to the actual sound of each bird in the story and the differences between these sounds.
- Invite a bird watcher to visit the classroom to share his or her experiences.

Observation: Notice how children distinguish between sounds made by different birds.

DAY 3 OBJECTIVES

CHILDREN WILL:

- listen for alliteration
- introduce the letter /kw/*qu*
- write letter *Qq*
- explore concepts of print: written and spoken words
- participate in a choral reading
- read the High-Frequency Reader: *We Like Fruit*
- identify the high-frequency word: *and*
- engage in Center Workshops

MATERIALS

- *Alphabatics*
- **High-Frequency Reader:** *We Like Fruit*
- **ABC Card:** *Qq*
- **My Alphabet Book, p. 19**
- **My Read and Write Book, pp. 21–23**

 The Big Book is available on audiocassette in the Literacy Place Listening Center.

My Alphabet Book, p. 19

Revisit the Big Book

 **DAILY PHONICS**

 and Read the High-Frequency Reader

Consonant /kw/qu

Ⓐ PHONOLOGICAL AWARENESS

Alliteration Say this alliterative sentence emphasizing the beginning sounds in the *Qq* words.

The queen quickly quit her quilting.

Then invite children to repeat it with you saying each word slowly and counting the number of times they hear **/kw/**. After children are comfortable with the sentence, have fun trying to say it quickly.

Ⓑ CONNECT SOUND-SPELLING

Introduce Consonant /kw/qu Page through *Alphabatics* chanting the alphabet until you get to the *Qq* page. Point out to children that the letters *Qu, qu* stand for the sounds **/kw/** heard at the beginning of **quail.** Show the ABC Card for *Qq.* Have children name the letter and the picture.

Letter Formation

WRITE THE LETTER

Write *Qq* on the chalkboard. Point out the capital and small forms of the letter. Model how to write the letter using the rhymes provided.

- Have children write both forms of the letter. Ask children to make the letter's sound as they practice writing. Note their posture, pencil grip, and paper position as they write.

Q	q
Make a great big circle and when you're done, *(Draw large circle.)* **Have that circle stick out its tongue.** *(Draw slanted line at bottom right of circle.)*	**Make a circle, add a stick,** *(Draw circle. Pull it straight down below base line.)* **At the bottom, give it a kick.** *(Pull down. Curve up.)*

Good-Night, Owl!

OPTIONS

Reread the Big Book

Story Pattern Read the book aloud, encouraging children to look for each of the creatures from the cover. Invite children to chime in with the sounds each creature makes.

Help children notice the story pattern.

▶ **How is each page the same?**

Guide children to recognize how the first line tells the creature's name and the second line has sound words. Point out that "and Owl tried to sleep" is repeated in the same place on each page.

Setting Discuss how the setting and time of day are important parts of the story.

▶ **What kind of information do the pictures give you about where these creatures live?**

▶ **Why are daytime and nighttime important in the story? How do the pictures help you know what time of day it is?**

READ AND
WRITE
INDEPENDENTLY

Journal Place copies of *Good-Night, Owl!* and the audiocassette in the Reading Center. Children can write about sounds in their own environment.

Concepts of Print

MATCH
SPEECH TO
WRITTEN
WORD

Reread the first page, tracking the print. Invite children to identify the repeated sound word and to come up and frame it. As each sound word is identified, write it on a chart under the heading "Sound Words." Have children repeat each sound and track the letters as they say them. Invite children to suggest other sounds for the chart.

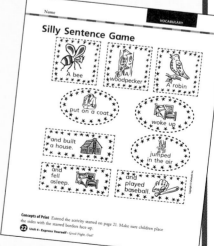

**My Read and Write Book,
pp. 21–22**

We Like Fruit

ESL/ELD

▲ Invite English language learners to draw a picture of each fruit named in *We Like Fruit*. Then guide them to label each piece of fruit in English and in their first language. **(MAKE CONNECTIONS)**

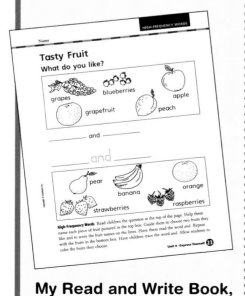

My Read and Write Book, p. 23

Read High-Frequency Reader

INTRODUCE THE BOOK

Show the book *We Like Fruit*. Read the title and the author's name. Explain that it tells a story about the kinds of fruit that different children like to eat.

▶ **What kinds of fruit do you like to eat? Where do you go shopping for fruit?**

HIGH-FREQUENCY WORD: and

Write the sentence *I like dogs and cats* on the board. Read it aloud. Review the high-frequency words *I* and *like* by asking volunteers to find them on the Word Wall. Underline the word *and*. Then write the word *and* on a note card. Read it aloud.

• Display the card and have children read the word.

• Help children spell it aloud, clapping on each letter.

• Ask children to write it in the air as they state aloud each letter.

Next, write the sentence stem *I like _____ and _____.* Invite children to complete the sentence stem by naming two things that they like. Write each new sentence on the board.

Add the card for *and* to the Word Wall.

SHARE THE HIGH-FREQUENCY READER

Read the story aloud, tracking the print. Invite children to point to the high-frequency word *and.*

After each two-page spread, ask: *Do you like this fruit?* Encourage children to name other food items that they have seen in a grocery store.

SHARED WRITING

Invite children to make a class book called *You and I.*

• Ask each child to name something they do with another person. Help children write and complete the sentence *You and I _____* on a piece of paper. Have them illustrate their sentences. Bind the pages into a book and share it with the class.

CENTER WORKSHOPS

Art

MATERIALS

- Corrugated cardboard
- Construction paper
- Paints and brushes
- Markers
- Scissors
- Double-stick tape

Owl's Tree

Work together using an old cardboard box to make a tree trunk and branches similar to Owl's tree. Set out art materials so that children can create living things for the tree. Some may want to make leaves. Others may want to make Owl and his fellow tree-dwellers.

Observation: Notice how children use the materials to illustrate life in the tree.

Math

MATERIALS

- Big Book of *Good-Night, Owl!*
- Chart paper
- Markers

How Many Animals?

Invite children to work together to tally the animals in *Good-Night, Owl!* in different ways. First they can count the number of each kind of creature that appears in the book, recording their findings with tally marks. Then, children can categorize the creatures according to the number of each kind shown on each page.

1—owl, squirrel, woodpecker, cuckoo, robin
2—crows, starlings, doves
3—jays
4—sparrows

Observation: How do children go about counting the animals?

DAY 4
OBJECTIVES

CHILDREN WILL:

- orally blend word parts
- review consonant /kw/qu
- read and respond to *Minerva Louise at School*
- discuss character
- identify setting
- write story extensions
- focus on sequence
- engage in Center Workshops

MATERIALS

- *Minerva Louise at School*
- **My Read and Write Book,** p. 24

Share the Read Aloud

DAILY PHONICS

Consonant /kw/qu

Ⓐ PHONOLOGICAL AWARENESS

Oral Blending State aloud the following word parts and ask children to blend them. Provide corrective feedback.

/kw/. . . een   /kw/. . . iet   /kw/. . . ail

/kw/. . . ick   /kw/. . . ack   /kw/. . . it

Ⓑ CONNECT SOUND-SPELLING

The Queen's Crown Remind children that the letters *qu* stand for **/kw/** as in **queen**. Invite children to suggest words that begin with **/kw/** and write each word on the chalkboard. Have volunteers circle the letter *q*.

Invite children to make **Qq** crowns out of construction paper. Help them write a *q* word on their crowns.

Build Background

ORAL LANGUAGE: SCHOOL

Invite children to look around the classroom and name some of the things they see. Write observations on a chart under the heading "Things in Our Classroom."

▶ **Which of these things do you usually find only in a classroom? Which of these things can you find at home?**

PREVIEW AND PREDICT

Read the title and the name of the author/illustrator of *Minerva Louise at School*. Display the cover and ask:

▶ **Who do you think Minerva Louise is? What will she do at school?**

SET A PURPOSE

Invite children to look for ways that the school in the book is like their own.

Share the Read Aloud

FOCUS ON SETTING

As you read try to capture the humor as Minerva Louise looks at everything in the classroom from a hen's perspective. Encourage children to look closely at the pictures to see why Minerva Louise imagines she is in a special kind of barn.

Respond to the Literature

TALK ABOUT IT

Share Personal Responses Encourage children to share their enjoyment of the story's humor.

▶ **What did you like about this story? Which parts did you think were especially funny?**

▶ **What do you think would have happened if Minerva Louise had run into someone at the school?**

▶ **Did the story turn out the way you thought it might from looking at the cover?**

Minerva Louise at School

THINK ABOUT IT

Explore Character Point out that Minerva Louise is a hen but that like many animal characters in stories, she has a lot of personality. Flip through the pages to guide children as they recall events that help the reader get to know her better.

▶ **Why does Minerva Louise visit the school?**

▶ **Would you like to be friends with Minerva Louise?**

▶ **Why do you think Minerva Louise changed the area where she lives after visiting the school? What does this tell you about the character?**

▶ **What would you tell other children about Minerva Louise?**

Try to guide children to use describing words and phrases such as *curious, funny, silly,* and *good imagination* when they talk about Minerva Louise. After your discussion, you may want to review some of the key words children used to describe Minerva Louise.

MODIFY Instruction

GIFTED & TALENTED

✳ **Invite children to write or dictate a sequel to the story. Ask them to imagine what would happen if Minerva Louise returned to the school when it was filled with children. (PREDICT)**

OBSERVATION

How are children doing? Are they:

- understanding the importance of sequence?
- using picture clues?
- enjoying humor and surprise?
- understanding the story's point of view?

My Read and Write Book, p. 24

Shared Writing

EXTEND THE STORY

Ask children to think of a different object that Minerva Louise might see in a classroom. Invite children to draw Minerva Louise with the new classroom object. Encourage children to use the "Things in Our Classroom" chart for ideas.

Help children label their drawings with the sentence "It looks like a _____." The last word should tell what Minerva Louise might imagine the object to be. Remind children to end the sentence with a period. Bind their pages into a book called *More Adventures with Minerva Louise.*

Repeated Reading

FOCUS ON SEQUENCE

Reread the story. Stop every few pages to have children review the order of events.

▶ **What is the first thing that happened in this story?**

▶ **What happened next?**

▶ **What is the last thing that happened?**

READ AND WRITE INDEPENDENTLY

Journal Place a copy of *Minerva Louise at School* in the Reading Center for children to look at independently or in small groups. You might suggest that children draw pictures in their Journals of other places Minerva Louise might visit.

✓ Comprehension Check

RETELL THE STORY

Invite volunteers to retell the story as you show the pictures. On each page encourage children to explain what Minerva Louise thinks she is seeing.

CENTER WORKSHOPS

Art

Create a Character

Give each child a sock. Provide markers and collage materials and invite children to decorate faces and bodies on their socks.

- Show children how to make their puppets move and talk.
- Invite children to think of a name and a personality for their puppet. Ask each child to tell you about their puppet, and write down what they say on a chart.
- Children can use their puppets to act out scenes.
- Display the puppets and the descriptions of them where everyone can see.

Observation: How do children describe their puppets?

MATERIALS

- **Socks**
- **Markers**
- **Collage material**
- **Chart paper**

Games

How Many Ways Can You Use It?

Invite children to work in small groups to play this game.

- Provide each group with one or two familiar objects.
- Challenge the group to take turns handling the objects and try to come up with many different ways they could be used.
- Have groups share their objects and ideas and write them down.
- Have children draw pictures to show their ideas.

Observation: Notice how children work together to come up with ideas.

MATERIALS

- **Assortment of ordinary objects from home or school such as kitchen utensils, stationery supplies, string, a pail, clothing**
- **Markers**
- **Chart paper**

CHILDREN WILL:

- generate rhyming words
- recognize sound letter relationships for /kw/qu
- review high-frequency words
- read My Book: *I Can Draw*
- engage in Center Workshops

MATERIALS

- *Big Book of Rhymes and Rhythms*, p. 22
- *Sentence Strips for "Q Was a Quail"*
- *Alphabatics; A Was Once an Apple Pie; Apples, Alligators and also Alphabets*
- ABC Card: *Qq*
- My Book: *I Can Draw*
- My Read and Write Book, p. 25

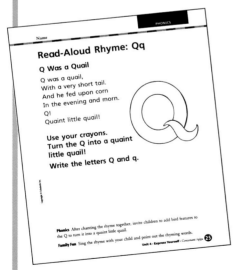

My Read and Write Book, p. 25

For additional practice see *Scholastic Phonics K*, pp. 91–94.

Sounds and Letters

Consonant /kw/qu

A **PHONOLOGICAL AWARENESS**

Rhyme Read aloud "Q Was a Quail" from the *Big Book of Rhymes and Rhythms*. Ask children what sound they hear at the beginning of *quail* and *quaint*. Explain the meaning of each word. Read the rhyme again, and invite children to join in. Have children think of new words that rhyme with *tail* and *quail*.

B **CONCEPTS OF PRINT**

Place the *Big Book of Rhymes and Rhythms,* the Sentence Strips for "Q Was a Quail," and a pocket chart in the Reading Center. Then do the following:

- Display the Sentence Strips. Have children place each strip where it belongs in the pocket chart.
- Write the letter **Qq** on an index card for each child.
- Read the poem slowly. Each time you say a word that begins with *Qq,* let children hold up their *Qq* cards.
- Repeat, asking children to point to the uppercase or lowercase letter in *Qq* word.
- Encourage children to notice the exclamation points.

Big Book of Rhymes and Rhythms, p. 22

> ### Q was a quail
>
> ### With a very short tail.

C CONNECT SOUND-SPELLING

Alphabetic Principle Show children the ABC card for *Qq.* Remind them that the letters **qu** stand for **/kw/** as in **queen.** Page through *Alphabatics* as children chant the letters of the alphabet. Briefly review the sound that each letter stands for, stopping on the letter **Qq.** Invite children to name the letter and say the sound.

ABC Book Explain to children that they are going to make a new page for their own ABC book. Have children suggest animals, objects, and people whose names begin with **/kw/.** Encourage children to notice that the letter **q** is always followed by a **u.** When the list is complete, invite children to work together to create the *Qq* page for their ABC Books.

ABC Book Hunt Display the alphabet books children have already read this year and others you might have in your classroom. Ask children to look at the pages for *Qq* in each book and to compare them. Are any of the words and pictures the same? Have children pick out other favorite letters to look for in each book. Encourage them to compare and contrast the objects pictured.

D VOCABULARY: HIGH-FREQUENCY WORDS

Display a block and a pencil. Write the sentence *I see a block and a pencil* on the board. Read it aloud. Then do the following:

- Review the high-frequency words. You may wish to use the read-spell-write-routine.
- Invite a volunteer to find two small classroom objects.
- Write the new sentence: "I see a _____ and a _____."
- Have children read the sentence and underline the word *and.*
- Repeat with other objects.

TECHNOLOGY

Use the **WiggleWorks Plus** Magnet Board activity to provide additional practice with words that begin with *Qq.* Children can write the word *quack* on the Magnet Board. Ask them to explode the word to scramble the letters. Encourage them to reassemble the word as quickly as they can.

The rhyme in the *Big Book of Rhymes and Rhythms* is available on the **Sounds of Phonics** audiocassette.

I Can Draw

EXTRA HELP

■ Invite children to draw a farm animal. Allow them to share their drawings with classmates. **(BUILD ON SUCCESS)**

Read My Book

INTRODUCE THE BOOK

Let children know they are going to get their own book that they can read on their own and take home.

▶ **What kinds of things do you like to draw or paint?**

PREVIEW AND PREDICT

Pass out copies of *I Can Draw*. Read the title and the author's and illustrator's names. Ask children about the illustration on the cover.

▶ **What do you think this boy is getting ready to do?**

▶ **What do you think this book might be about?**

READ TOGETHER

Read the My Book with children, tracking the print as you read. Have children identify the high-frequency words *I* and *can*. Guide children to read along in their copies and to think about the different drawings the boy is making.

PHONICS

Ask children to say the word *lamb* aloud.

▶ **What letter stands for the sound you hear at the beginning of the word?**

Encourage children to use other sound-spellings they have learned to read new words.

READ AND WRITE INDEPENDENTLY

Journal Encourage children to read *I Can Draw* on their own or in small groups. Provide crayons and invite children to color the illustrations.

HOME/SCHOOL CONNECTION

Children can take home their My Books to share with family members and friends. Suggest that children and family members work together to draw or paint their own farm scene.

CENTER WORKSHOPS

Health & Fitness

MATERIALS

- Tape recorder
- Index cards with the following phrases with rebus drawings: *move quickly, move quietly, move like a queen, move like an animal that quacks, move like a quail*

Qq Moves

Prepare the cards or tape-record sentences. One child can take a card and have a partner read the phrase, or a child can play the tape. Children can then move according to the instructions. Encourage them to use their entire bodies as they move.

After children act out all the directions, they can play again by choosing a card and asking the rest of the group to guess the phrase they are acting out.

Observation: Which *Qq* moves do children really enjoy? Which children learn about the letter *Qq* this way?

Alphabet

MATERIALS

- Feathers
- Trays with ink
- Writing or parchment paper

Qq's With Quills

Display a feather and talk about how people in the past used quills for writing. Let children examine the feathers and then experiment dipping the quills in ink (or paint) and making designs. Let children practice writing the letter *Qq*. Encourage them to write words with *Qq*.

Observation: Which words do children choose to write?

DAY 6 OBJECTIVES

CHILDREN WILL:

- build phonological awareness
- recognize /r/
- listen and respond to *The Spider Weaver*
- talk about narrative folk tales
- recognize story sequence
- engage in Center Workshops

MATERIALS

- My Read and Write Book, pp. 26–27

GUIDED READING

To conclude each day's reading session, meet with guided reading groups. You might use Scholastic's Guided Reading Library or other books in your library.

TECHNOLOGY

 Children can get practice with "mouse control" by viewing the animated storybooks at **www.billybear4kids.com**.

 The song is available on the **Sounds of Phonics** audiocassette.

Storytelling Circle

DAILY PHONICS

Consonant /r/r

PHONOLOGICAL AWARENESS

Repetition Read aloud the title "Row, Row, Row Your Boat." Ask children how many times the word *row* is repeated. Ask whether they think the title "Row Your Boat" would be as much fun.

- Invite children to say the title of the song with you as you exaggerate the beginning /r/ sound in *row*.
- Then sing or play the song. Invite children to join in during a second singing. Have them emphasize the initial sound in *row*.

Row, Row, Row Your Boat

Row, row, row your boat
Gently down the stream
Merrily, merrily, merrily, merrily
Life is but a dream.

READ Aloud

The Spider Weaver

A Folk Tale from Japan
retold by Florence Sakade

Long ago there was a young farmer named Yosaku. One day he was working in the fields and saw a snake getting ready to eat a spider. Yosaku felt very sorry for the spider. So he ran at the snake with his hoe and drove the snake away, thus saving the spider's life. Then the spider disappeared into the grass, but first it seemed to pause a minute and bow in thanks toward Yosaku.

One morning not long after that, Yosaku was in his house when he heard a tiny voice outside calling: "Mr. Yosaku, Mr. Yosaku." He went to the door and saw a beautiful young girl standing in the yard.

"I heard that you are looking for someone to weave cloth for you," said the girl. "Won't you please let me live here and weave for you?"

Build Background

ORAL LANGUAGE: CLOTHES

Explain that the folk tale *The Spider Weaver* is from Japan and that it tells about a spider who weaves cloth into beautiful robes called *kimono*. Invite children to share what they know about how clothes are made. You may want to mention words such as *weaving, sewing,* and *knitting.*

Tell the Story

FOCUS ON THE ORAL TRADITION

Tell or read the story with expression. As you read, encourage children to use their knowledge of folk tales to predict and understand story events. After the young girl first appears ask:

▶ **Who do you think this girl really is?**

▶ **Why do you think she is offering to weave?**

Respond to the Literature

TALK ABOUT IT

Share Personal Responses Provide time for children to share their wonderings and interest.

▶ **Have you ever heard a story like this? How was it similar?**

▶ **What if Yosaku had not peeped in the window?**

▶ **Would you have peeped in the window?**

MODIFY Instruction

ESL/ELD

▲ Create simple drawings of the main characters—Yosaku, the farmer, the snake, the spider, the girl, and Old Man Sun. Identify each character and have students repeat the name. As you read, hold up the appropriate picture each time you mention a character's name. **(USE VISUALS)**

Yosaku was very pleased because he did need a weaving girl. So he showed the girl the weaving room and she started to work at the loom. At the end of the day Yosaku went to see what she'd done and was very surprised to find that she'd woven eight long pieces of cloth, enough to make eight kimono. He'd never known anyone could weave so much in just a single day.

"How ever did you weave so much?" he asked the girl.

But instead of answering him, she said a very strange thing: "You mustn't ask me that. And you must never come into the weaving room while I am at work."

But Yosaku was very curious. So one day he slipped very quietly up to the weaving room and peeped in the window. What he saw really surprised him! Because it was not the girl who was seated at the loom, but a large spider, weaving very fast with its eight legs, and for thread it was using its own spider web, which came out of its mouth.

Yosaku looked very closely and saw that it was the same spider which he'd saved from the snake. Then Yosaku understood. The spider had been so thankful that it had wanted to do something to help Yosaku. So it had turned itself into a beautiful young girl and come to weave cloth for him. Just by eating the cotton in the weaving room it could spin it into thread inside its own body, and then with its eight legs it could weave the thread into cloth very, very fast.

My Read and Write Book, pp. 26–27

THINK ABOUT IT Recognize Sequence Guide children to understand the events of the story by asking them to participate in drawing a story map on a piece of mural paper. Invite children to draw key events of the story as you list them on a chart.

Shared Writing

WRITE STEPS IN A PROCESS Remind children of what the spider did with its weaving skills. Invite them to tell how the spider wove the cloth. Ask what the spider did first. Then ask what it did next. Write down what children say. Then have them help you order the steps by writing a number before each sentence. Have children choose one step to draw and label.

Retell the Story

GROUP RETELLING Retell *The Spider Weaver*. Invite children to tell parts of it by asking "What happened next?" after each episode. Tie a long piece of yarn into a circle for children to hold as they tell the story.

✓ Comprehension Check

ACT IT OUT Meet with several groups of children to discuss how they would like to act out the story of *The Spider Weaver*. Entertain their ideas for props and actors. Be prepared to narrate the story again while they dramatize it or to refer to the chart you made during Think About It.

READ Aloud

continued from page T127

Yosaku was very grateful for the spider's help. He saw that the cotton was almost used up. So next morning he set out for the nearest village, on the other side of the mountains, to buy some more cotton. He bought a big bundle of cotton and started home, carrying it on his back.

Along the way a terrible thing happened. Yosaku sat down to rest, and the same snake that he'd driven away from the spider came up and slipped inside the bundle of cotton. But Yosaku didn't know anything about this. So he carried the cotton home and gave it to the weaving girl.

She was very glad to get the cotton, because she'd now used up all the cotton that was left. So she took it and went to the weaving room.

As soon as the girl was inside the weaving room she turned back into a spider and began eating the cotton very, very fast, just as though it

CENTER WORKSHOPS

Art

MATERIALS

- **Cotton balls and batting**
- **Mural paper**
- **Paints**
- **Glue**

Weaving Cloud Pictures

Take children outside to watch clouds. Ask them to look for shapes like the ones that the spider weaver wove in the story.

Provide children with plenty of paper on which they can paint and draw sky scenes. Encourage them to glue cotton to the paper to create fleecy, white clouds.

When they are finished, ask children to describe their clouds to a friend. Place the mural on a bulletin board or wall to share with other classes and family members.

Observation: How do children incorporate the events of the story into their cloud formations?

were something very delicious, so she could spin it into thread inside her body. The spider ate and ate and ate, and then suddenly, when it had eaten down to the bottom of the bundle the snake jumped out of the cotton. It opened its mouth wide to swallow the spider. The spider was very frightened and jumped out the window. The snake went wriggling very fast after it. And the spider had eaten so much cotton that it couldn't run very fast. So the snake gradually caught up with the spider. Again the snake opened its mouth wide to gulp the spider down. But just then a wonderful thing happened.

Old Man Sun, up in the sky, had been watching what was happening. He knew how kind the spider had been to Yosaku and he felt very sorry for the poor little spider. So he reached down with a sunbeam and caught hold of the end of the web that was sticking out of the spider's mouth, and he lifted the spider high up into the sky, where the snake couldn't reach it at all.

The spider was very grateful to Old Man Sun for saving it from the snake. So it used all the cotton that was inside its body to weave beautiful fleecy clouds up in the sky. That's the reason, they say, why clouds are soft and white like cotton, and also that is the reason why both a spider and a cloud are called by the same name in Japan—*kumo*.

DAY 7 OBJECTIVES

CHILDREN WILL:

- listen for alliteration
- recognize consonant /r/r
- write letter *Rr*
- talk about the SourceCard
- write stories about pictures
- recognize a sentence
- revisit High-Frequency Reader: *We Like Fruit*
- engage in Center Workshops

MATERIALS

- ABC Card: *Rr*
- *Creative Expression*, SourceCard 3
- High-Frequency Reader: *We Like Fruit*
- My Alphabet Book, p. 20

TECHNOLOGY

Build words that contain the letter *Rr* in the **WiggleWorks Plus** Magnet Board. Guide children to frame the letter *Rr* everywhere they see it.

My Alphabet Book, p. 20

Read the SourceCard

and Read the High-Frequency Reader

Consonant /r/r

Ⓐ PHONOLOGICAL AWARENESS

Alliteration Read the following alliterative sentence aloud: ***Roberto and Randy raced in the rain.***

Then read the sentence again, very slowly, emphasizing each **/r/** sound.

Ⓑ CONNECT SOUND-SPELLING

Introduce Consonant /r/r Page through *Alphabatics* until you get to the *Rr* page. Point out to children that the letter *Rr* stands for **/r/** as in *rooster*. Ask children to say the sound **/r/** with you.

- Say the word *rooster* again and ask children to exaggerate **/r/** at the beginning of the word.

Display an ABC Card for *r*. Have children say the name of the letter and the word that begins with *r*.

Letter Formation

WRITE THE LETTER

Write *Rr* on the chalkboard. Point out the capital and small forms of the letter. Model how to write each form, using the rhymes provided below.

- Have children write both forms of the letter in the air with their fingers. Ask children to make the letter's sound as they practice writing.

R	r
Make a long straight line, strong and tall. *(Pull down straight. Lift and begin again at top.)* **Add a bump and a ladder leaning against the wall.** *(Curve around. Slant down from curve to bottom.)*	**Make a short straight line starting halfway down.** *(Pull down straight. Lift.)* **Go back to the top and add a little crown.** *(At the top, make the beginning of a curve.)*

Share the SourceCard

SIDE ONE   **Cat Tales** Show the art masterpieces portraying cats and give children time to examine each one. Point out the labels written in French, Japanese, Chinese, and English and ask children what they think each word means.

▶ **What is the same about these words? What is different?**

Invite children to study each image of a cat.

▶ **How was each piece of art made? What materials and tools did the artist need?**

▶ **Which cat looks most realistic?**

▶ **What is each cat doing? What stories do you think the artists were trying to tell?**

SIDE TWO   **Explore the Art Process** Invite children to guess what the girl in the pictures is doing. Read the phrase at the top of the SourceCard. Remind children of the four pieces of cat art they saw on side one of the SourceCard.

▶ **How did this girl make her picture of a cat? What tools and materials did she use?**

▶ **What do the numbers written next to each picture tell you?**

▶ **Why do you think the girl painted a cat? What story do you think she is trying to tell with her painting?**

Shared Writing

WRITE STORIES ABOUT PICTURES   Give children the opportunity to practice spelling and writing the word *cat*. Encourage children to write stories to accompany the cat art on side one of the SourceCard by writing letters for the sounds they know.

Ask children to share their stories with one another. How are their stories the same? How are they different? Bind the stories into a class cats book.

MODIFY Instruction

ESL/ELD

▲ After reviewing the cat labels on side one of the SourceCard, invite children whose first language is not represented in the labels to share the word for *cat* in their first language. **(MAKE CONNECTIONS)**

We Like Fruit

MODIFY Instruction

ESL/ELD

▲ Use visuals to introduce all the fruit names before reading the book *We Like Fruit.* Ask children which fruit is their favorite. If possible, ask them to bring their favorite fruit to class. **(USE VISUALS)**

Revisit High-Frequency Reader

REREAD THE BOOK

Invite children to join you as you read the book *We Like Fruit* again. On the third page, have children read the words in the sentence that they already know (*I, like, and*). Review these words.

DECODING STRATEGIES

As you go through the book, point to each word, the initial letter, any other sound-spellings children have learned, and the picture clue. Pause long enough for children to read before you do. Model blending words as needed. For example, have children use their knowledge of /p/p to decode *pears.*

Think Aloud *At the beginning of the word, I see the letter* p. *I know that* p *stands for* /p/. *In the picture I see* pears. *The word* pears *begins with* /p/. *This word is* pears. *That makes sense in the sentence.*

CONCEPTS OF PRINT: MATCH WORDS

Give partners two Sentence Strips. Cut across the dotted lines and mix up the words. Invite children to reconstruct the sentences by matching the words to the words in the book.

ORAL LANGUAGE: FAVORITE FRUITS

Have children review which fruits the children in the story like. Then ask them to name other fruits.

- On chart paper, list each fruit mentioned in the story and the fruits the children name. Invite children to draw a picture of each fruit next to its name.

READ WITH A PARTNER

Give each child their own copy of *We Like Fruit.*

- Have children read their books with a partner. Partners can take turns reading the pages. Have them name the color of each fruit.

READ AND WRITE INDEPENDENTLY

Journal Place copies of the High-Frequency Reader in the Reading Center for children to read on their own. Children can draw or write in their Journals about fruits they like.

HOME/SCHOOL CONNECTION

Children can take home their High-Frequency Reader and work with family members on a new book about what they like to eat.

CENTER WORKSHOPS

Art

MATERIALS

- Clay
- Paint, brushes
- Paper
- Blocks
- Collage materials
- Glue, scissors
- Markers or crayons

Mixed Media

Encourage small groups of children to choose one animal or object for everyone in the group to portray. Suggest that each child pick his or her own materials and tools.

As the groups finish their artwork, set up a museum corner to display their work. Encourage children to write labels for their work. Invite children from other classes to view the museum exhibit.

Observation: How do children personalize their artwork?

Games

MATERIALS

- Index cards
- Crayons or markers

Sort the Steps

Invite children to think of something they do that involves several steps, such as cooking, building with blocks, or getting bundled up for playing in the snow. Children can list the steps on a sheet of scrap paper.

- Encourage children to draw and label pictures to show each step, using one index card for each step.
- Children can mix up the order of their set of cards, and then exchange them with a partner to reorder.

Observation: Notice how children break a process down into separate steps.

DAY 8
OBJECTIVES

CHILDREN WILL:

- orally blend onset and rime
- review consonant /r/r
- blend words with *-an*
- listen and respond to *Whistle for Willie*
- write sentences about shadows
- recognize sequence
- engage in Center Workshops

MATERIALS

- *Whistle for Willie*

Share the Read Aloud

Consonant /r/r

Ⓐ PHONOLOGICAL AWARENESS

Oral Blending State aloud the following word parts, and ask children to blend them. Provide corrective feedback.

/r/ . . . an	/r/ . . . ake	/r/ . . . ope
/r/ . . . ing	/r/ . . . ain	/r/ . . . ose

Ⓑ CONNECT SOUND-SPELLING

A Row of Roses Draw a row of flower stems. Write the word *rose* on the top of a stem and circle the letter *r.* Remind children that the letter *r* stands for /r/. Invite children to suggest words that begin with /r/. Write each word on the chalkboard, and have volunteers circle the letter *r* and draw a rose around each word.

Ⓒ BLEND

List the following words and sentence on the chalkboard. Have children read each word and sentence aloud chorally. Model blending where necessary.

- ran
- fan
- man
- The man ran.

Build Background

ORAL LANGUAGE: LEARNING NEW THINGS

Ask children to think about learning how to do new things such as tying their shoelaces or doing a somersault.

► **What did you learn to do? What was hard about learning how to do it?**

► **How did it feel to learn something new?**

PREVIEW AND PREDICT

Read the title of the book, tracking the print. Point out that the author and illustrator is the same person. Invite children to look at the cover of the book.

► **What do you think the boy is trying to do?**

► **What is the dog doing?**

Share the Read Aloud

FOCUS ON ILLUSTRATIONS
As you read the story encourage children to look closely at the pictures and point out the details they notice in the colorful and imaginative artwork.

• Guide children to notice how colors and shapes are used in each setting.

Whistle for Willie

Respond to the Literature

TALK ABOUT IT
Share Personal Responses Allow children some time to share their responses to both the artwork and the story.

▶ What was your favorite part of the story?

▶ How do you think Peter felt when he was trying to learn how to whistle? Have you ever felt like that when you tried to learn something new?

▶ What did you like about the pictures in the story?

▶ How did the pictures help make the story more interesting?

THINK ABOUT IT
Focus on Theme Ask children to think about how hard Peter tried to whistle.

▶ Why do you think he kept trying?

▶ How do you think he would feel if he gave up?

▶ If Peter learned how to whistle the first time he tried, how would the story be different? Would you like it better?

▶ If Peter never learned to whistle, what else could he have done to get his dog's attention?

GIFTED & TALENTED

☀ Invite children to create a variation on the story by having Peter learn how to do something else. **(INNOVATE)**

SING A SONG
Invite children to sing and whistle along to the song, "Whistle While You Work."

☀ DAY 8

TEACHER TIP

To keep children who cannot whistle from feeling discouraged, invite them to share a different talent.

MODIFY Instruction

EXTRA HELP

■ Some children might benefit from brainstorming a list of words that describe their shadow before they write their sentences. **(BRAINSTORM)**

Shared Writing

WRITE SHADOW SENTENCES

Invite children to explore their own shadows just like Peter does in the story. Shine a flashlight and encourage children to try moving in front of the light in different ways to see how their shadows move. Ask children to write sentences about their shadows.

Write the following sentences on the chalkboard:

My shadow is tall and wavy.

My shadow looks like a tree.

Help children complete sentences by writing what their shadow looks like. Invite them to draw a picture of their shadows.

Repeated Reading

RECOGNIZE SEQUENCE

Reread the story, asking children to listen for the different ways Peter tries to learn how to whistle.

▶ **Where is Peter the first time he tries to whistle?**

▶ **What is he doing the next time he tries to whistle? Does it work?**

Continue asking about Peter's different attempts to whistle as you continue reading.

READ AND WRITE INDEPENDENTLY

Journal Place copies of *Whistle for Willie* in the Reading Center for children to read independently or with a partner. Invite children to write and draw in their Journals about something else Peter could do to get his dog's attention while he is learning to whistle.

☑ Comprehension Check

ACT IT OUT

Invite children to role-play the different characters as you retell the story. When you finish, invite children to try whistling. Encourage children to help each other.

CENTER WORKSHOPS

Art

MATERIALS

- Scrap materials
- Old wallpaper books
- Construction paper
- Scissors
- Glue
- *Whistle for Willie*

Make Pictures With Collage Materials

Put *Whistle for Willie* in the Art Center so that children can study the individual pictures.

Spend some time talking with children about how the pictures were made. Help them realize that the pictures are constructed from wallpaper, lace, and newspaper, which was cut in shapes and glued on paper.

Encourage children to use the scraps to make their own pictures.

Observation: Notice how carefully children examine Ezra Jack Keats's collages while they are creating their own.

Dramatic Play

MATERIALS

- Large cardboard box
- Small boxes

A Box Is...

Let children explore the possibilities of a box. Put the large box in the dramatic Play Center and invite children to pretend that it's a car, ship, train, spaceship, and anything else they can imagine.

Invite children to make or find props to use in their play, such as hats for their different roles.

Add small boxes and let children put them together to create new structures.

Observation: What do children create with their boxes?

DAY 9 OBJECTIVES

CHILDREN WILL:

- recognize sound-spelling relationship for /r/r
- review phonogram *-an*
- review high-frequency words
- read My Book: *We Like to Build*
- engage in Center Workshops

MATERIALS

- *Big Book of Rhymes and Rhythms,* p. 23
- ABC Card: *Rr*
- Sentence Strips for "Ride a Cock-Horse"
- *Good-Night, Owl!*
- *My Read and Write Book,* p. 28

My Read and Write Book, p. 28

For additional practice see *Scholastic Phonics K,* pp. 95–98. See also Sound and Letter Book: *I Read.*

Sounds and Letters

and Read My Book

Consonant /r/r

A PHONOLOGICAL AWARENESS

Rhyme Read aloud "Ride a Cock-Horse" from the *Big Book of Rhymes and Rhythms.* Ask children what sound they hear at the beginning of the words *ride* and *rings.* Invite children to repeat the words as you exaggerate the beginning sound. Encourage children to notice the rhyming words.

B CONCEPTS OF PRINT

Place the *Big Book of Rhymes and Rhythms,* the Sentence Strips for "Ride a Cock-Horse," and a pocket chart in the Reading Center. Then do the following:

- Read the rhyme together, asking children to "ride a horse" in place in time with the rhythm.
- Reread the rhyme again, one line at a time. Ask volunteers to find the Sentence Strip for each line and place it in the pocket chart.
- Invite volunteers to frame each word in a sentence with their fingers.
- Then have children point to all of the words that begin with *Rr.*

Big Book of Rhymes and Rhythms, p. 23

Ride a cock-horse

To Banbury Cross,

To see a fine lady

Upon a white horse.

C CONNECT SOUND-SPELLING

Alphabetic Principle Remind children that the letter *r* stands for **/r/** as in *ring*. Reread the page from *Good-Night, Owl!* where all the animals make noise. Invite children to repeat the *rat-a-tat* sound of the woodpecker. Have them frame the letter *r* in *rat-a-tat*. Repeat for the word *robin*.

ABC Book Explain to children that they are going to make a new page for their own ABC book. Have children suggest animals, objects, and people whose names begin with **/r/.** When the list is complete, invite children to work together to create the **Rr** page for their ABC Books.

The Man Ran Write the phonogram **-an** on the chalkboard. Remind children that the phonogram **-an** stands for **/an/** as in the word **man.** Add the letters **m, c, d, f, p,** and *r* and have children blend the words formed. Model blending as necessary.

Invite children to dictate sentences with as many *-an* words as they can. Encourage children to illustrate their *-an* sentences.

D VOCABULARY: HIGH-FREQUENCY WORDS

Draw children's attention to the high-frequency Word Wall. Review the words children have learned so far this year.

- Ask volunteers to find a word you name. Then use the read-spell-write method as you point to each word card.
- Place the high-frequency word cards in a pocket chart.
- Help children to make new sentence stems by combining the word cards. Have the class suggest words to complete each new sentence stem.

The Nature of Systematic Instruction in Beginning Reading

Systematic instruction in beginning reading follows a scope and sequence for building, reviewing, and applying content of phonological awareness, phonics, and high-frequency sight word knowledge. Instruction (a) progresses from easier to more difficult activities, (b) is direct and explicit, and (c) follows a predictable daily routine.

TECHNOLOGY

Place the letters *AN* on the **WiggleWorks Plus** Magnet Board. Invite children to choose a letter to place before *AN* to make a word that means *moved very fast.* **(RAN)** Have children make other *-AN* words.

The rhyme from the Big Book of Rhymes and Rhythms is available on the **Sounds of Phonics** audiocassette.

We Like to Build

MODIFY Instruction

ESL/ELD

▲ Invite children to use the blocks from the Block Center to act out the sequence of events in *We Like to Build*. Guide children to review sequence by asking: *What did you do first? Next? Last?* (SEQUENCE)

Read My Book

INTRODUCE THE BOOK

Let children know that they are going to get their own book that they can read on their own and take home.

▶ **What are some of the things you play with when you are in school?**

▶ **Is there anything in school that you can use to build things?**

PREVIEW AND PREDICT

Pass out copies of *We Like to Build*. Read the author's and illustrator's names.

▶ **What do you think these children are going to do? What might this book be about?**

READ TOGETHER

Read My Book with children, tracking the print as you read. Have children identify the high-frequency words *I, like,* and *to*. Guide children to read along in their copies and to notice how the children in the story work together to make something grow.

PHONICS

Ask children to say the word *build* aloud.

▶ **What letter stands for the sound you hear at the beginning of the word?**

READ AND WRITE INDEPENDENTLY

Journal Encourage children to read *We Like to Build* on their own or in small groups. Provide crayons and invite children to color the illustrations.

HOME/SCHOOL CONNECTION

Children can take home their My Book to share with family members and friends. Suggest that children work with a family member to build their own city out of blocks, cardboard boxes, or other materials.

CENTER WORKSHOPS

Science

Rocks, Rivers, and Rainbows

There are many objects and events in nature whose names begin with *Rr*. Let children come up with their own list of nature words such as *rock, river, rainbow, rain,* and *rose*. Then they can illustrate words from the list in little blank books, titling their work "My Little *Rr* Nature Book."

Observation: Which children really like making their own books and using picture dictionaries to come up with new ideas?

MATERIALS

- ABC books
- Children's picture dictionaries
- Little blank books
- Markers
- Crayons

Math

Rock Count

Invite children to paint an uppercase *R* on one side of each rock and a lowercase *r* on the other side. Then pairs of children can play a counting game. Place the rocks in a box or bowl. One child shakes the container and pours out the rocks. That child scores one point for each uppercase letter and two points for each lowercase letter that appears. Children keep score for each round by using counters or by tallying.

Observation: Watch to see if children change the game in any way or come up with their own *Rr* game.

MATERIALS

- Five small, smooth rocks
- Paints
- Small box or bowl

Put It All Together

Sum It Up

DISCUSS STORIES

Remind children that they have been reading about different story characters who discovered they could do funny or surprising things. Display all the books children have read in the last nine days. Encourage children to talk about the stories. In what ways are they alike? In what ways are they different? How did the ending of each book show something surprising about each main character?

ORAL LANGUAGE: POEM

Read the poem "Surprise" together.

▶ **What do you think the author meant by the "hidden you?" Have you found the "hidden you" in any of the books we've read?**

Invite children to draw a picture of a story character they feel is like them. Have them talk about their pictures.

Surprise

**The biggest
Surprise
On the library shelf
Is when you suddenly
Find yourself
Inside a book—
(The hidden you)
You wonder how
The author knew.**

Beverly McLoughland

Language Experience Chart

COMPARE
AND
CONTRAST
CHART

Display the books that children have shared. Review the books and talk together about the art in each one.

▶ **How did the author or characters use art?**

Work together to make a language chart showing how the stories used art. The chart might look like the one shown.

Display the chart as part of the documentation of the work children have done.

MODIFY
Instruction

EXTRA HELP

■ Before creating the chart, you might help children refresh their memories by asking them to brainstorm words, characters, and sounds they remember from each story. Organize their ideas on a chart and talk about each word they suggest.
(GRAPHIC DEVICE)

Stories and Art

Good-Night, Owl!	Minerva Louise at School	Whistle for Willie	The Spider Weaver
The author tells a story with beautiful pictures.	Minerva Louise sees things differently and makes us look at the pictures in a new way.	The author uses colors, shapes, and real-life objects to show different places.	The spider creates a beautiful cloth.

Observation:

Listen as children talk about the stories they've shared.

• Are they talking about their favorite stories?

• Are they relating story details?

• Are they recognizing how the stories are alike?

DAY 10

MODIFY Instruction

ESL/ELD

▲ Model the position of the tongue near, but not touching, the top of the mouth when making the sound /r/. Have children acquiring English look in a mirror as they practice the sound. Be aware that children who speak Spanish may tend to roll, or trill, the sound /r/, while children who speak Asian languages may confuse it with the sound /l/. **(MODEL)**

DAILY PHONICS

Maintenance

Ⓐ PHONOLOGICAL AWARENESS

Rhyme Grab Bag Collect objects with names that rhyme with other common words. For example: a pen, a can, a box, a rock, a glass, a top, a hat, and a ball.

• Place the objects in a bag.

• Invite children to come up and take an object out of the bag.

• Say the object's name slowly. Then challenge the class to think of words that rhyme with the object's name.

Ⓑ PHONICS ACTIVITY

Rabbit's Rocket Draw a picture of a large rocket on chart paper and label it with the words *Rabbit's rocket*. Have children point to the letter *Rr* at the beginning of *Rabbit* and *rocket* and say the sound it stands for.

Then tell children that Rabbit is going on a trip in his rocket. Invite them to name things that begin with the sound **/r/** that Rabbit might take along with him on his trip. *(rope, rattle, radio, ring, rock, rose, rug, ruler, roller skates)*

Write the words children suggest inside the rocket. When they have finished, read the items and invite children to illustrate them.

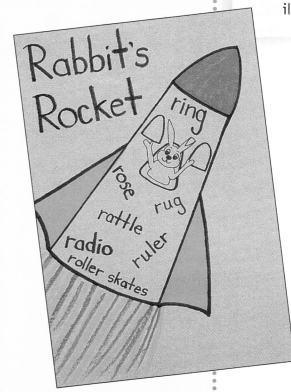

WEEKS 5 AND 6
PROJECT

Meet the Authors

Applaud the children's creativity by having a Meet the Authors Celebration, during which children will write about themselves and their writing experiences. As part of the celebration, place an author's chair in the room, and let children sit in it when they read their stories to the group.

Invite family members to the Meet the Authors Celebration. Display all of the books children have created throughout the Creative Expression Unit. Encourage children to read and talk about the books.

Remind children of the Meet the Mentor Video they saw about author Pat Mora. Let children know they can work together to write a book about some very creative authors—themselves!

Children can interview a partner about his or her writing experiences as the other children listen. Write down the partner's responses on a chart. Help children generate a list of interview questions. Questions might include:

▶ **What kinds of stories do you like to write?**

▶ **Do you have a favorite place to write? Where?**

▶ **What do you use to write? Do you like to use pencils or markers? Do you like to use a paper or a computer?**

When everyone has been interviewed, let children illustrate their pages. Ask children to dictate a few sentences about themselves which can be included in a brief biographical statement on the back cover. If possible include a photo of the authors, too. Staple all of the sheets of chart paper together. Make a cover, writing the title "Meet the Authors," and listing children's names.

Display the "Meet the Authors" book along with the other books children have created.

MATERIALS

- **Chart paper**
- **Markers**
- **Photographs of children (optional)**
- **My Read and Write Book, pp. 31–32**

BENCHMARKS

Monitor children's progress. Are they

- expressing themselves clearly?

- identifying story characters and making comparisons?

- seeing themselves as authors?

TEACHER RESOURCES
BIBLIOGRAPHY

Books for Sharing

✳ **Cultural Connection**   ★ **Kid Picks**   🦋 **Science**   🌐 **Social Studies**   🧮 **Math**   🎭 **The Arts**

WEEKS 1 AND 2

Baby-O
by Nancy White Carlstrom
illustrated by Sucie Stevenson
Little, Brown & Co. Inc.,
1992 🌐 ✳
A family loads its jitney bus,
Baby-O, for market day in
the West Indies in this
rhythmically told tale.

Barnyard Banter
by Denise Fleming
Henry Holt & Co., 1994 ★
Readers will enjoy rhyming
barnyard noises and hide-
and-seek with Goose.

City Noise
by Karla Kuskin
illustrated by Renee Flower
HarperCollins, 1994 🎭 🌐
Noises and colorful paintings
create a lively urban scene.

The First Song Ever Sung
by Laura Melmed
illustrated by Ed Young
Lothrop, Lee & Shepard
Books, 1993 ✳
People and animals tell a
young boy their own idea of
what the first song was, in
this story set in ancient
Japan.

Small Green Snake
by Libba M. Gray
illustrated by Holly Meade
Orchard Books, 1994 ★ 🎭
A small snake hisses his way
into and out of trouble in
this playful story.

Who Says Moo?
by Muriel and Lionel Kalish
Scholastic Inc., 1993 ★
This whimsical barnyard book
is full of animal sounds.

WEEKS 3 AND 4

Miranda's Day to Dance
by Jackie Jasina Schaefer
Atheneum Publishers, 1994
🎭
Miranda dances to thank the
animals for the fruit they
bring her.

Rat-a-Tat, Pitter Pat
by Benjamin Alan
photographed by
Margaret Miller
HarperCollins, 1987 🎭
Photographs show sounds
and actions.

Silent Lotus
by Jeanne M. Lee
Farrar, Straus & Giroux Inc.,
1991 🎭 ✳
Though unable to speak or
hear, Lotus learns the com-
plex dances of Cambodian
ballet.

**The Three Little Pigs and
the Fox**
by William Hooks
illustrated by Steve Schindler
Macmillan Publishing Co.,
1989 ✳
Children will enjoy this
Appalachian variant of the
familiar story.

Together
by George Ella Lyon
illustrated by Ver Rosenberry
Orchard Books, 1989 ★
Two best friends share imaginative adventures.

WEEKS 5 AND 6

At the Beach
by Huy Voun Lee
Henry Holt & Co., 1994
🎭 ✳
Xiao Ming's mother shows
him some Chinese characters
during a day at the beach.

Moving to Town
by Mattie Lou O'Kelley
Joy Street Books, 1991
🎭 🌐
Detailed folk-art paintings
tell the story of a family's
move in the early 1900s.

**Nine-in-One Grr! Grr! A
Folktale from the Hmong
People of Laos**
by Blia Xiong
illustrated by Nancy Horn
Scholastic Inc., 1994 🎭 ✳
This tale of a clever bird out-
foxing tigers is depicted in
the style of traditional
Hmong embroidery.

The Story of a Farm
by John Goodall
McElderry Books, 1979
🎭 🌐
Watercolor paintings show the
history of an English farm.

**Tye May and the Magic
Brush**
by Molly Bang
Greenwillow Books, 1981 ✳
In this Chinese tale, what-
ever Tye May paints with her
brush becomes real.

The Yellow Umbrella
by Henrik Drescher
Bradbury Press, 1987 🎭
Two monkeys fly in a word-
less adventure, beautifully
and gently illustrated.

Books With Phonic Elements

Martha the Movie Mouse
by Arnold Lobel
HarperCollins, 1966
Martha saves the show
and gets top billing on
the marquee. (M)

Noisy Nora
by Rosemary Wells
Dial, 1973
Nora is noisy because she
wants attention from her
busy family. (N)

The Owl and the Pussycat
by Edward Lear
illustrated by Jan Brett
Scholastic Inc., 1995
Edward Lear's classic poem is
accompanied by lush illustrations showing life above and
under the water on the owl
and the pussycat's journey. (O)

The Piggy in the Puddle
by Charlotte Pomerantz
illustrated by James Marshall
Macmillan Publishing Co., 1974
Children will be pleased by
this poem about a pig (and
parents) and a puddle. (P)

The Quilt Story
by Tony Johnston
illustrated by Tomie dePaola
Scholastic Inc., 1993
A quilt links two little girls
across generations. (Q)

Rain
by Robert Kalan
illustrated by Donald Crews
Greenwillow Books, 1978
This energetic book shows the
many colors before, during,
and after a rainstorm. (R)

Books in Other Languages

Spanish

Canto una canción
by Cecilia Avalos
illustrated by Glen Davis
Scholastic Inc., 1993

A girl sings of the desert and what makes it special, in a story written in Spanish.

El toro pinto and Other Songs in Spanish
by Anne Rockwell
Simon & Schuster, 1995

This lively collection of traditional songs from Spanish-speaking lands offers lyrics in Spanish and English.

Silba por Willie
by Ezra Jack Keats
Viking, 1992
Peter wants to learn to whistle so he can call his dog, Willie.

Chinese

Grandma Moses of Taiwan
by Su Chengming
illustrated by Su Yango
Multicultural Distribution Center, 1991
Chinese text and plenty of illustrations show Grandma Su painting the sights of rural Taiwan.

Japanese

Whistle for Willie
by Ezra Jack Keats
Multicultural Distributing Center
A careful Japanese translation tells how Peter wants to learn to whistle so he can call his dog, Willie.

Author Study: Pat Mora

The Desert Is My Mother
by Pat Mora
illustrated by Daniel Lechon
Arte Público Press, 1994

Mora poetically describes the desert as the source of many things in this bilingual English/Spanish story.

The Race of Toad and Deer
by Pat Mora
illustrated by Maya Itzna Brooks
Orchard Books, 1995
In this Guatemalan folk tale, Toad races Deer—and gets some help from his friends.

Tomás and the Library Lady
by Pat Mora
Alfred A. Knopf Inc., 1996
Tomás returns to the library every year on his travels with his migrant-worker family.

Teacher's Bookshelf

Chants
by Pat Mora
Arte Público Press, 1994
This collection of poems evokes the Southwest and the author's Mexican-American culture.

The Migration Series
by Jacob Lawrence
Rappahannock Press, 1993
Dozens of paintings chronicle the great migration of African Americans from the South to the urban North.

Nepantla
by Pat Mora
Arte Público Press, 1995
A collection of personal essays provides insight into this author's life, writing, and creative process.

The People Speak: Navajo Folk Art
by Chuck and Jan Rosenak
photographed by Lynne Lowe
Northland Publishing Co., 1994
More than 100 works by Navajo artists appear in this collection.

Technology

For more information about Scholastic's technology, call 1-800-SCHOLASTIC

Software

WiggleWorks Plus
Scholastic (Win/Mac)
This CD-ROM component for Kindergarten through Grade 2 of Literacy Place supports children's language development. Its activities integrate reading, writing, listening, and speaking.

I Spy
Scholastic (Win/Mac)
These scavenger-hunt games build reading, math, problem-solving, and logic skills.

Scholastic Reading Counts!
(Formerly "The Electronic Bookshelf") This reading motivation/management program is for students at all reading levels.

Usborne's Animated First Thousand Words
Usborne/Scholastic (Win/Mac)
This vocabulary tool introduces pre- and beginning readers to English and Spanish words.

Huggly's Sleepover: I'm Ready for Kindergarten
Scholastic (Win/Mac)
The first software with a complete balance of essential skills for Kindergarten.

Internet

www.scholasticnetwork.com
This comprehensive online curriculum service for grades K–8 features unit-by-unit extensions for Literacy Place.

www.scholastic.com
Scholastic's corporate web site includes Literacy Place resources and unit-related Internet links.

Other Sites
The Internet is growing and changing every day, so be sure to preview all sites before your students visit them.

Scope and Sequence

GRADE	K	1	2	3	4	5
READING						
Print Awareness						
recognize that print messages represent spoken language and conveys meaning	●	●				
knows print moves left-right, top-bottom	●	●				
understands that written words are separated by spaces	●	●				
know the difference between individual letters and words	●	●				
know the difference between capital and lower-case letters	●	●				
know the order of the alphabet	●	●				
recognize conventions of capitalization and punctuation	●	●				
understand that spoken words are represented in written language by specific sequences of letters	●	●				
recognize parts of a book	●	●	●	●	●	●
recognize that there are correct spellings	●	●	●	●	●	●
recognize distinguishing features of paragraphs			●	●	●	●
Phonological Awareness						
divide sentences into individual words	●	●	●			
identify, segment, and combine syllables	●	●	●	●		
produce and distinguish rhyming words from non-rhyming	●	●	●	●		
identify and isolate initial and final sounds	●	●	●	●		
blend sounds	●	●	●	●		
segment one-syllable words into individual phonemes clearly producing beginning, medial, and final sounds	●	●	●	●		
Letter–Sound Relationships						
name and identify each letter of the alphabet	●	●				
understand that written words are composed of letters that represent sounds	●	●				
learn and apply letter-sound correspondences of:						
consonants (beginning, middle, end)	●	●	●			
short vowel sounds	●	●	●			
phonograms/word families/patterns	●	●	●			
digraphs		●	●	●	●	●
blends		●	●	●	●	●
long vowel sounds		●	●	●	●	●
diphthongs		●	●	●	●	●
variant vowels		●	●	●	●	●
blend initial letter-sounds with common vowel spelling patterns to read words	●	●	●	●		
decode by using all letter-sound correspondences within regularly spelled words	●	●	●	●	●	●
use letter-sound knowledge to read decodable texts	●	●	●	●		

● = direct instruction   = mastery

Grade	K	1	2	3	4	5
Word Identification						
decode by using all letter-sound correspondences within a word	●	●	●	●	●	●
use common spelling patterns to read words	●	●	●	●	●	●
use structural cues to recognize compounds, base words, and inflectional endings		●	●	●	●	●
use structural cues to recognize prefixes and suffixes			●	●	●	●
use root words and other structural cues to recognize derivational endings			●	●	●	●
identify multisyllabic words by using common syllable patterns			●	●	●	●
recognize high-frequency irregular words	●	●	●	●	●	●
use knowledge or syntax and context to support word identification and confirm meaning	●	●	●	●	●	●
read regular and irregular words automatically		●	●	●	●	●
locate meanings, pronunciations, and derivations of unfamiliar words using dictionaries, glossaries, and other sources		●	●	●	●	●
Fluency						
read regularly in independent-level materials		●	●	●	●	●
read regularly in instructional-level materials		●	●	●	●	●
read orally from familiar texts		●	●	●	●	●
self-select independent-level materials		●	●	●	●	●
read silently for increasing amounts of time		●	●	●	●	●
demonstrate characteristics of fluent and effective reading		●	●	●	●	●
adjust reading rate based on purpose		●	●	●	●	●
read aloud		●	●	●	●	●
Text Structures/Literary Concepts						
distinguish different forms of texts	●	●	●	●	●	●
understand simple story structure	●	●	●	●	●	●
distinguish fiction from nonfiction	●	●	●	●	●	●
distinguish fact from fantasy	●	●	●	●	●	●
distinguish among types of text	●	●	●	●	●	●
distinguish between roles of the author and illustrator	●	●	●	●	●	●
identify text as narrative or expository			●	●	●	●
compare communication in different forms	●	●	●	●	●	●
understand and identify literary terms	●	●	●	●	●	●
analyze characters	●	●	●	●	●	●
identify importance of setting	●	●	●	●	●	●
recognize and analyze story problem/plot and resolution	●	●	●	●	●	●
judge internal consistency or logic of stories and texts		●	●	●	●	●
recognize that authors organize information in specific ways		●	●	●	●	●

✸ Scope and Sequence

GRADE	K	1	2	3	4	5
identify purposes of different types of texts	●	●	●	●	●	●
recognize the distinguishing features of genres		●	●	●	●	●
describe the author's perspective or point of view			●	●	●	●
Variety of Texts						
read fiction, nonfiction, and poetry for pleasure and information	●	●	●	●	●	●
use graphs, charts, signs, captions and other informational texts to acquire information	●	●	●	●	●	●
read classic and contemporary works	●	●	●	●	●	●
read from print a variety of genres for pleasure and information	●	●	●	●	●	●
read from electronic sources a variety of genres for pleasure and information	●	●	●	●	●	●
read to accomplish various purposes		●	●	●	●	●
select varied sources, i.e., nonfiction, novels, textbooks, newspapers and magazines for information and pleasure		●	●	●	●	●
read for varied purposes, i.e., to be informed, entertained, appreciate writer's craft, and discover models for writing		●	●	●	●	●
Vocabulary Development						
discuss meanings and develop vocabulary through meaningful/concrete experiences	●	●	●	●	●	●
develop vocabulary by listening and discussing selections read aloud	●	●	●	●	●	●
identify words that name persons, places or things, and actions	●	●	●	●	●	●
use dictionaries, glossaries, technology, and context to build word meanings and confirm pronunciation		●	●	●	●	●
demonstrate knowledge of synonyms, antonyms and multiple-meaning words		●	●	●	●	●
draw on experiences to bring meanings to words in context		●	●	●	●	●
use thesaurus, synonym finder, dictionary and software to clarify meanings and usage				●	●	●
determining meanings of derivatives by applying knowledge of root words and affixes		●	●	●	●	●
use curricular content areas and current events to study words			●	●	●	●
Comprehension						
use prior knowledge and experiences	●	●	●	●	●	●
establish purposes for reading	●	●	●	●	●	●
retell or act out the order of events in stories	●	●	●	●	●	●
monitor own comprehension		●	●	●	●	●
draw, discuss, and describe visual and mental images		●	●	●	●	●
make and explain inferences, i.e., determining important ideas, causes and effects, making predictions, and drawing conclusions		●	●	●	●	●
identify similarities and differences in topics, characters, problems, and themes	●	●	●	●	●	●
produce summaries of text selections		●	●	●	●	●
represent text information through story maps, graphs, charts, outline, time line, or graphic organizer	●	●	●	●	●	●

● = direct instruction   ▧ = mastery

Grade	K	1	2	3	4	5
distinguish fact from opinion			●	●	●	●
practice different kinds of questions and tasks, including test-like questions		●	●	●	●	●
use cause and effect, or chronology to locate and recall information		●	●	●	●	●
determine main idea and supporting details	●	●	●	●	●	●
paraphrase and summarize text	●	●	●	●	●	●
draw inferences and support with text evidence and experience		●	●	●	●	●
find similarities and differences across texts in treatment, scope, organization		●	●	●	●	●
answer different types and levels of questions, i.e., open-ended, literal, and interpretative; multiple-choice, true-false, and short-answer	●	●	●	●	●	●

Literary Response

	K	1	2	3	4	5
listen to stories read aloud	●	●	●	●	●	●
participate actively during a read aloud of predictable and patterned selections	●	●	●	●		
respond through talk, movement, music, art, drama, and writing	●	●	●	●	●	●
describe how illustrations contribute to text	●	●	●	●	●	●
connect, compare, and contrast ideas, themes, and issues across texts	●	●	●	●	●	●
demonstrate understanding of informational texts through writing, illustrating, demonstrations	●	●	●	●	●	●
support interpretations or conclusions with examples from text		●	●	●	●	●
offer observations, make connections, react, speculate, interpret, and raise questions in response to text	●	●	●	●	●	●
interpret texts through journal writing, discussion, enactment, and media	●	●	●	●	●	●
support responses by referring to relevant aspects of the text and own experiences	●	●	●	●	●	●

Inquiry/Research

	K	1	2	3	4	5
identify and form relevant questions for research	●	●	●	●	●	●
use pictures, print, and people to gather and answer questions	●	●	●	●	●	●
draw conclusions from information gathered	●	●	●	●	●	●
locate and use important areas of the library/media center	●	●	●	●	●	●
use alphabetical order to locate information		●	●	●	●	●
recognize and use parts of a book to locate information	●	●	●	●	●	●
use multiple sources to locate information that addresses questions			●	●	●	●
interpret and use graphic sources of information, i.e., charts, graphs, and diagrams	●	●	●	●	●	●
demonstrate learning through productions and displays	●	●	●	●	●	●
organize information in systematic ways		●	●	●	●	●
use compiled information and knowledge to raise additional unanswered questions				●	●	●
use text organizers to locate and organize information			●	●	●	●
summarize and organize information from multiple sources by taking notes, outlining ideas, or making charts			●	●	●	●

Scope and Sequence

GRADE	K	1	2	3	4	5
Culture						
connect own experiences with life experiences, language, customs, and cultures of others	●	●	●	●	●	●
compare experiences of characters across cultures	●	●	●	●	●	●
compare text events with own and other readers' experiences	●	●	●	●	●	●
determine distinctive and common characteristics of cultures through wide reading	●	●	●	●	●	●
articulate and discuss themes and connections that cross cultures	●	●	●	●	●	●
LISTENING/SPEAKING						
determine purposes	●	●	●	●	●	●
respond to directions and questions	●	●	●	●	●	●
participate in rhymes, songs, conversations and discussions	●	●	●	●	●	●
listen critically to interpret and evaluate	●	●	●	●	●	●
listen to stories and other texts read aloud	●	●	●	●	●	●
identify musical elements of literary language	●	●	●	●	●	●
connect experiences and ideas with those of others	●	●	●	●	●	●
compare language and oral traditions that reflect customs, regions, and cultures	●	●	●	●	●	●
choose appropriate language for audience, purpose, and occasion	●	●	●	●	●	●
use verbal and nonverbal communication when making announcements, directions, introductions	●	●	●	●	●	●
ask and answer relevant questions, and contribute	●	●	●	●	●	●
present dramatics	●	●	●	●	●	●
gain control of grammar	●	●	●	●	●	●
learn vocabulary of school	●	●	●	●		
use vocabulary to describe ideas, feelings, and experiences	●	●	●	●	●	●
support spoken language using props	●	●	●	●	●	●
retell by summarizing or clarifying	●	●	●	●	●	●
eliminate barriers to effective listening	●	●	●	●	●	●
understand major ideas and supporting evidence	●	●	●	●	●	●
interpret messages, purposes, and perspectives	●	●	●	●	●	●
identify and analyze persuasive techniques			●	●	●	●
distinguish between opinion and fact				●	●	●
monitor own understanding		●	●	●	●	●
listen to proficient models of oral reading	●	●	●	●	●	●
describe how language of literature affects listener	●	●	●	●	●	●
assess language choice and delivery				●	●	●
identify how regional labels/sayings reflect regions and cultures				●	●	●
demonstrate skills that reflect interviewing, reporting, requesting and providing information		●	●	●	●	●

● = direct instruction   = mastery

Grade	K	1	2	3	4	5
use effective rate, volume, pitch, tone	●	●	●	●	●	●
give precise directions and instructions in games and tasks	●	●	●	●	●	●
clarify and support with evidence, elaborations and examples		●	●	●	●	●

WRITING

Penmanship/Capitalization/Punctuation

	K	1	2	3	4	5
write own name and other important words	●	●				
write each letter of alphabet, capital and lowercase	●	●				
use phonological knowledge to map sounds to letters, in order to write messages	●	●	●	●	●	●
write messages left to right, top to bottom	●	●	●	●		
gain control of pencil grip, paper position, beginning strokes, posture, letter formation, appropriate size, and spacing	●	●				
use word and letter spacing and margins		●	●			
use capitalization and punctuation, i.e., names, first letters in sentences, periods, question marks, exclamation marks, proper nouns, abbreviations, commas, apostrophes, quotation marks, contractions, possessives	●	●	●	●	●	●
write legibly by selecting cursive or manuscript, as appropriate		●	●	●	●	●

Spelling

	K	1	2	3	4	5
write with proficient spelling of: CVC, CVC silent e, one syllable with blends		●	●	●	●	●
inflectional endings: plurals, verb tenses, drop final e when endings are added			●	●	●	●
single-syllable words with r-controlled vowels, final consonants		●	●	●	●	●
orthographic patterns, i.e., consonant doubling, dropping e, changing y to i			●	●	●	●
use resources to find correct spellings, synonyms, and replacements			●	●	●	●
use conventional spelling of familiar words in final drafts		●	●	●	●	●
spell multisyllabic words using regularly spelled phonogram patterns			●	●	●	●
write with more proficient spelling of contractions, compounds, and homonyms		●	●	●	●	●
open and closed syllables, consonant before -le, and syllable boundary patterns			●	●	●	●
spell words ending in -tion and -sion				●	●	●
spell accurately in final drafts		●	●	●	●	●

Composition/Process

	K	1	2	3	4	5
dictate messages	●	●	●			
write labels, notes, and captions for illustrations, possessions, charts, and centers	●	●	●	●	●	●
write to record ideas and reflections	●	●	●	●	●	●
generate ideas before writing on self-selected topics	●	●	●	●	●	●
generate ideas before writing on assigned topics	●	●	●	●	●	●
develop drafts		●	●	●	●	●
use available technology to compose text	●	●	●	●	●	●
revise selected drafts for varied purposes		●	●	●	●	●
revise drafts for coherence, progression, and logical support of ideas		●	●	●	●	●

Scope and Sequence

GRADE	K	1	2	3	4	5
edit for appropriate grammar, spelling, punctuation, and features of polished writings		●	●	●	●	●
demonstrate understanding of language use and spelling by bringing pieces to final form and "publishing"		●	●	●	●	●
proofread own writing and that of others		●	●	●	●	●
select and use reference materials and resources for writing		●	●	●	●	●
Purposes						
dictate messages	●	●	●			
write labels, notes, and captions for illustrations, possessions, charts, and centers	●	●	●	●	●	●
write to record ideas and reflections	●	●	●	●	●	●
write to express, discover, record, develop, reflect, and refine ideas, and to problem solve	●	●	●	●	●	●
write to communicate with a variety of audiences	●	●	●	●	●	●
write in different forms for different purposes	●	●	●	●	●	●
write to influence			●	●	●	●
write to inform	●	●	●	●	●	●
write to entertain	●	●	●	●	●	●
exhibit an identifiable voice in personal narratives and stories			●	●	●	●
choose the appropriate form for own purpose for writing				●	●	●
use literary devices, i.e., suspense, dialogue, figurative language			●	●	●	●
Grammar/Usage/Mechanics						
use nouns and verbs in sentences	●	●	●	●	●	●
compose complete sentences and use appropriate punctuation	●	●	●	●	●	●
use singular and plural forms of regular nouns		●	●	●	●	●
compose sentences with interesting elaborated subjects				●	●	●
edit writing toward standard grammar and usage		●	●	●	●	●
use correct irregular plurals			●	●	●	●
use singular and plural forms of regular nouns, and adjust verbs for agreement		●	●	●	●	●
compose elaborated sentences and use appropriate punctuation				●	●	●
use regular and irregular plurals correctly			●	●	●	●
write in complete sentences, varying the types			●	●	●	●
employ standard English usage, subject-verb agreement, pronoun referents, and parts of speech		●	●	●	●	●
use adjectives and adverbs		●	●	●	●	●
use prepositional phrases to elaborate written ideas				●	●	●
use conjunctions to connect ideas				●	●	●
use apostrophes in contractions and possessives		●	●	●	●	●
use objective-case pronouns accurately			●	●	●	●

● = direct instruction   = mastery

	GRADE	K	1	2	3	4	5
Evaluation							
identify the most effective features of a piece by using student and teacher criteria			●	●	●	●	●
respond constructively to others' writing		●	●	●	●	●	●
determine how own writing achieves its purposes			●	●	●	●	●
use published pieces as models		●	●	●	●	●	●
review collection of own work to monitor growth			●	●	●	●	●
apply criteria to evaluate writing			●	●	●	●	●
review a collection of written works to determining its strengths and weaknesses, and to set goals			●	●	●	●	●
Inquiry/Research							
record/dictate questions for investigating		●	●	●	●	●	●
record/dictate own knowledge		●	●	●	●	●	●
take simple notes from sources			●	●	●	●	●
compile notes into outlines, reports, summaries				●	●	●	●
frame questions, to direct research			●	●	●	●	●
organize prior knowledge with graphic organizer		●	●	●	●	●	●
take notes from various sources				●	●	●	●
summarize and organize ideas			●	●	●	●	●
present information in various forms		●	●	●	●	●	●
evaluate own research and raise new questions					●	●	●
Connections							
collaborate with other writers			●	●	●	●	●
correspond with peers or others by e-mail or conventional mail					●	●	●
VIEWING							
Representing/Interpretation							
describe illustrator's choice of style, elements, and media		●	●	●	●	●	●
interpret events and ideas from maps, charts, graphics, video segments, and technology presentations		●	●	●	●	●	●
Representing/Analysis							
interpret and evaluate visual image makers		●	●	●	●	●	●
compare-contrast print, visual, and electronic media		●	●	●	●	●	●
Representing/Production							
select, organize, and produce visuals to complement and extend meanings		●	●	●	●	●	●
produce communications using technology		●	●	●	●	●	●

Index

GRADE K

This index incorporates references to the Teacher's Edition for all six units in Grade K of Literacy Place. For your convenience, the index is divided into three sections, as listed below.

Index

SKILLS AND STRATEGIES

References to the book you're in are in blue. Each unit in Grade K is identified by the initials of its theme.

PV · Personal Voice: Stories About Us

PS · Problem Solving: See It, Solve It

TW · Teamwork: All Together Now!

CE · Creative Expression: Express Yourself

MI · Managing Information: I Spy!

CI · Community Involvement: Join In!

Recognize Literary Genres

CE: T14–T16, T60–T62, T106–T108; **MI:** T14–T16, T60–T62, T106–T108; **CI:** T14–T16, T60–T62, T106–T108

Concept Book, PV: T118–T120; **PS:** T64–T66, T68–T69; **TW:** T18–T20, T22–T23; **MI:** T26–T28, T64–T66, T68–T69, T72–T74; **CI:** T80–T82

Information, PV: T18–T20, T22–T23, T110–T112, T114–T115; **TW:** T110–T112, T127–T128; **MI:** T18–T20, T22–T24, T88–T90, T118–T120; **CI:** T18–T20, T22–T24, T26–T28

Photo Essay, MI: T18–T20, T22–T23, T126–T128

Poetry

Poetry/Song, PV: T14, T18, T26, T30, T34, T35, T46, T50, T62, T64, T72, T76, T80, T92, T96, T110, T118, T122, T134, T138, T142; **PS:** T18, T30, T34, T35, T39, T46, T64, T76, T80, T92, T110, T118, T122, T126, T138, T142; **TW:** T18, T23, T30, T34, T46, T65, T76, T92, T110, T122, T126, T138, T142; **CE:** T18, T28, T30, T46, T50, T76, T80, T92, T122, T138, T142; **MI:** T30, T34, T46, T61, T64, T76, T80, T110, T111, T122, T126, T138, T142; **CI:** T18, T30, T34, T46, T50, T76, T80, T92, T122, T126, T138, T142

Recognize Narrative Forms

Cumulative Story, PS: T80–T82; **TW:** T80–T82; **CE:** T110–T112, T114–T115

Predictable Story, PV: T34–T35, T42–T43, T64–T66, T68–T69; **PS:** T34–T35, T80–T82, T110–T112, T114–T115, T131, T143–T144; **CE:** T18–T20, T22–T23, T34–T36, T110–T112, T114–T115, T88–T90; **MI:** T110–T112, T114–T115, T126–T128; **CI:** T42–T44, T110–T112, T114–T115

Circular Story, PS: T64–T66, T68–T69; **CI:** T42–T44

Vocabulary

Collect Interesting Words, PV: T24; **PS:** T30, T47, T60, T61, T77, T93, T106, T107, T123, T139; **TW:** T14, T15, T31, T47, T60, T61, T62, T77, T93, T128, T136; **CE:** T14, T15, T31, T47, T82, T93, T123, T139; **MI:** T14, T15, T16, T17, T31, T38, T47, T77, T93, T123, T139; **CI:** T31, T47

Facial Expressions/Body Language, PV: T111, T112, T115, T120, T128; **PS:** T74, T75, **TW:** T72, T74; **CE:** T65, T66, T85, T87; **CI:** T74, T117

High-Frequency Words, PV: T24, T31, T40, T47, T70, T77, T86, T93, T116, T123, T132, T139; **PS:** T24, T31, T40, T47, T70, T77, T86, T93, T116, T123, T132, T139; **TW:** T24, T31, T40, T47, T70, T77, T93, T116, T123, T132, T139, T144; **CE:** T24, T31, T40, T47, T70, T77, T86, T93, T116, T123, T130, T132, T139; **MI:** T24, T31, T40, T47, T70, T77, T86, T93, T116, T123, T132, T139; **CI:** T24, T31, T40, T47, T70, T77, T86, T93, T116, T123, T132, T139

Make Word Categories, PV: T46, T70, T86, T114; **PS:** T14, T15, T87, T106, T121; **TW:** T14, T99, T141; **CE:** T41, T52, T111, T117; **MI:** T19, T33, T107; **CI:** T94

Story Vocabulary, PV: T20, T40, T44, T61, T65, T72, T86, T107; **PS:** T42, T61, T108; **TW:** T31, T35, T37, T93, T127, T139; **CE:** T16, T31, T43, T47; **MI:** T47, T61, T77; **CI:** T69

Writing and Language Arts Skills and Strategies

Conventions of Language

Mechanics

Capitalize First Word of Sentence, PV: T74; **PS:** T23, T123, T132; **TW:** T23, T40, T112, T132; **CE:** T132; **MI:** T28, T62, T69; **CI:** T16, T22, T23, T98, T122, T144

Punctuation

Exclamation Mark, PV: T66, T74; **TW:** T122; **CE:** T28, T122; **MI:** T69, T86; **CI:** T30

Period, PV: T74; **PS:** T23, T69; **TW:** T122; **CE:** T120, T132; **MI:** T66, T69, T132; **CI:** T16, T40, T86, T98, T122, T131, T132, T144

Question Mark, PV: T74; **PS:** T20, T23, T69, T123; **TW:** T86, T122, T131; **CE:** T86; **MI:** T66, T69, T132; **CI:** T31, T40, T76, T86, T98, T122, T131, T132, T144

Listening

Demonstrate Active Listening Skills

Follow Directions, PV: T22, T38, T46, T109, T121, T137; **PS:** T50, T90; **TW:** T63, T85, T87, T93, T113, T121, T127, T145; **CE:** T125; **MI:** T39, T41, T64, T79, T99

Listen to a Story/Poem, PV: T14, T15, T18, T19, T26–T27, T30, T34, T35, T42–T43, T46, T50, T62, T64, T67, T72–T73, T76, T80, T81, T85, T88–T89, T92, T96, T110, T118–T119, T134–T135, T138, T142; **PS:** T18, T26–T27, T30, T34, T35, T39, T42–T43, T46, T52, T64, T72–T73, T76, T80, T88–T89, T92, T110, T118–T119, T122, T126, T134–T135, T138, T142; **TW:** T26–T27, T42–T43, T64, T72–T73, T80, T88–T89, T96, T110, T118–T119, T131, T134–T135, T138; **CE:** T26–T27, T30, T34, T42–T43, T46, T50, T72–T73, T88–T89, T118–T119, T126, T134–T135; **MI:** T26–T27, T34, T42–T43, T46, T64, T72–T73, T76, T88–T89, T96, T118–T119, T134–T135, T138, T142; **CI:** T18, T26–T27, T34, T42–T43, T50, T72–T73, T76, T80, T88–T89, T92, T118–T119, T122, T126, T134–T135, T142

Listen to Each Other, to Others, and the Teacher

PV: T14, T15, T18, T19, T22, T23, T24, T26, T27, T30, T31, T34, T35, T38, T42, T43, T46, T47, T60, T61, T64, T65, T68, T69, T70, T72, T73, T74, T76, T77, T80, T81, T86, T88, T89, T92, T96, T106, T107, T110, T111, T114, T118, T119, T126, T127, T134, T135

PS: T14, T15, T18, T19, T22, T23, T24, T26, T27, T30, T31, T34, T35, T42, T43, T46, T47, T60, T61, T64, T65, T68, T69, T72, T73, T74, T76, T77, T80, T81, T86, T88, T89, T92, T106, T107, T110, T111, T114, T118, T119, T126, T127, T134, T135

TW: T14, T15, T18, T19, T22, T23, T24, T26, T27, T30, T31, T34, T35, T42, T43, T46, T47, T60, T61, T64, T65, T68, T69, T72, T73, T74, T76, T77, T80, T81, T86, T88, T89, T92, T106, T107, T110, T111, T114, T118, T119, T126, T127, T134, T135

CE: T14, T15, T18, T19, T22, T23, T24, T26, T27, T30, T31, T34, T35, T42, T43, T46, T47, T60, T61, T64, T65, T68, T69, T72, T73, T74, T76, T77, T80, T81, T86, T88, T89, T92, T106, T107, T110, T111, T114, T118, T119, T126, T127, T134, T135

Index

T44, T62, T66, T70, T74, T82, T85, T90, T108, T112, T116, T120, T128, T131, T136

Write With Symbols That Resemble Letters and Letter Shapes, PS: T30, T47, T60, T61, T77, T93, T106, T107, T123, T139; **TW:** T14, T15, T31, T47, T60, T61, T62, T77, T93, T128, T136; **CE:** T14, T15, T31, T47, T82, T93, T123, T139; **MI:** T14, T15, T16, T17, T31, T38, T47, T77, T93, T123, T139; **CI:** T31, T47

Speaking

Demonstrate Speaking Skills

Do a Commercial, TW: T62

Engage in Conversation by Sharing Ideas

PV: T14, T15, T18, T19, T22, T23, T24, T26, T27, T30, T31, T34, T35, T39, T41, T42, T43, T46, T47, T49, T50, T53, T60, T61, T64, T65, T68, T69, T72, T73, T74, T76, T77, T80, T81, T85, T86, T88, T89, T92, T96, T106, T107, T110, T111, T114, T118, T119, T126, T127, T134, T135

PS: T14, T15, T18, T19, T22, T23, T24, T26, T27, T30, T31, T34, T35, T42, T43, T46, T47, T52, T60, T61, T62, T64, T65, T66, T68, T70, T72, T73, T75, T77, T78, T80, T81, T86, T88, T89, T92, T106, T107, T110, T111, T114, T118, T119, T126, T127, T134, T135

TW: T14, T15, T18, T19, T22, T23, T24, T26, T27, T30, T31, T34, T35, T42, T43, T46, T47, T60, T61, T64, T65, T68, T69, T72, T73, T74, T76, T77, T80, T81, T86, T88, T89, T92, T106, T107, T110, T111, T114, T118, T119, T126, T127, T134, T135

CE: T14, T15, T18, T19, T22, T23, T24, T26, T27, T30, T31, T34, T35, T42, T43, T46, T47, T60, T61, T64, T65, T68, T69, T72, T73, T74, T76, T77, T80, T81, T86, T88, T89, T92, T106, T107, T110, T111, T114, T118, T119, T126, T127, T134, T135

MI: T14, T15, T18, T19, T22, T23, T24, T26, T27, T30, T31, T34, T35, T42, T43, T46, T47, T60, T61, T64, T65, T68, T69, T72, T73, T74, T76, T77, T80, T81, T86, T88, T89, T92, T106, T107, T110, T111, T114, T118, T119, T126, T127, T134, T135

CI: T14, T15, T18, T19, T22, T23, T24, T26, T27, T30, T31, T34, T35, T42, T43, T46, T47, T60, T61, T64, T65, T68, T69, T72, T73, T74, T76, T77, T80, T81, T86, T88, T89, T92, T106, T107, T110, T111, T114, T118, T119, T126, T127, T134, T135

Give Directions, PV: T38, T91; **TW:** T87, T99, T117

Orally Present Poetry, PV: T26, T34, T35, T36, T37, T46, T67, T72, T118; **PS:** T73, T76, T92, T112, T125, T126, T139; **TW:** T14, T31, T60, T136, T139; **CE:** T14, T31, T35, T36, T37; **MI:** T31, T47, T60, T106

Participate in Choral Reading, PV: T36, T62; **PS:** T69, T115; **TW:** T16, T35, T44; **CE:** T23, T26, T36, T62, T112; **MI:** T74, T128; **CI:** T115, T128

Participate in Echo Reading, PV: T35; **TW:** T115; **CE:** T19, T20, T35, T44, T64, T111; **MI:** T117; **CI:** T19, T81

Recite a Chant, PV: T26, T34, T35, T36, T37, T46, T67, T72, T118; **PS:** T73, T112, T132, T139; **TW:** T14, T31, T60, T123, T136, T139; **CE:** T14, T31, T35, T36, T37, T47, T95, T123; **MI:** T31, T47, T60, T106; **CI:** T31, T123

Role Play, PV: T20, T21, T41, T71, T82, T87; **PS:** T79; **TW:** T33, T35, T37, T74, T120, T129; **CE:** T29, T44, T82, T87, T136, T137; **MI:** T40; **CI:** T26, T63, T70, T108, T120, T137

Share Experiences

PV: T14, T15, T18, T19, T27, T39, T40, T64, T65, T71, T81, T83, T84, T89,

T91, T111, T118, T127

PS: T35, T43, T61, T65, T73, T81, T89, T111, T118, T119, T127, T135

TW: T15, T19, T27, T35, T43, T61, T65, T73, T81, T89, T127, T135

CE: T15, T18, T19, T20, T24, T25, T26, T27, T29, T32, T34, T35, T39, T40, T43, T58

MI: T15, T19, T27, T35, T42, T61, T65, T73, T127, T131, T135

CI: T15, T19, T27, T35, T36, T43, T61, T65, T73, T81, T89, T107, T111, T119, T127, T131, T135

Sing a Song, PV: T14, T30, T34, T50, T76, T79, T110; **PS:** T34, T39, T46, T64, T76, T110, T142; **TW:** T18, T34, T39, T50, T64, T80, T96, T106, T110, T126, T142; **CE:** T18, T26, T28, T34, T47, T51, T64, T80, T85, T92, T95, T96, T106, T108, T110, T126; **MI:** T18, T26, T30, T34, T64, T76, T110, T126; **CI:** T18, T34, T38, T53, T84, T85, T93, T96, T99, T111, T122, T127, T128, T145

Speak in Complete Sentences, PV: T14, T15, T18, T20, T22, T34, T35, T37, T38, T39, T42, T43, T44, T47, T49, T51, T64, T66, T67, T68, T69, T70, T71, T75, T77, T81, T86, T88, T89, T92, T106, T107, T110, T111, T114, T118, T119, T126, T127, T134, T135; **PS:** T14, T15, T18, T19, T22, T23, T24, T26, T27, T30, T31, T34, T35, T42, T43, T46, T47, T60, T61, T64, T65, T68, T69, T72, T73, T74, T76, T77, T80, T81, T86, T88, T89, T92, T106, T107, T110, T111, T114, T118, T119, T126, T127, T134, T135; **TW:** T14, T15, T18, T19, T22, T23, T24, T26, T27, T30, T31, T34, T35, T42, T43, T46, T47, T60, T61, T64, T65, T68, T69, T72, T73, T74, T76, T77, T80, T81, T86, T88, T89, T92, T106, T107, T110, T111, T114, T118, T119, T126, T127, T134, T135; **CE:** T14, T15, T18, T19, T22, T23, T24, T26, T27, T30, T31, T34, T35, T42, T43, T46, T47, T60, T61, T64, T65, T68, T69, T72, T73, T74, T76, T77, T80, T81, T86, T88, T89, T92, T106, T107, T110, T111, T114, T118, T119, T126, T127, T134, T135; **MI:** T14, T15, T18, T19, T22, T23, T24, T26, T27, T30, T31, T34, T35, T42, T43, T46, T47, T60, T61, T64, T65, T68, T69, T72, T73, T74, T76, T77, T80, T81, T86, T88, T89, T92, T106, T107, T110, T111, T114, T118, T119, T126, T127, T134, T135; **CI:** T14, T15, T18, T19, T22, T23, T24, T26, T27, T30, T31, T34, T35, T42, T43, T46, T47, T60, T61, T64, T65, T68, T69, T72, T73, T74, T76, T77, T80, T81, T86, T88, T89, T92, T106, T107, T110, T111, T114, T118, T119, T126, T127, T134, T135

Speak to Take a Telephone Message, PV: T49

Tell/Retell a Story, PV: T28, T37, T67, T69, T82, T83, T85, T90, T97, T131; **PS:** T20, T51, T52, T62, T65, T74, T82, T99, T119, T120, T128; **TW:** T16, T28, T44, T82; **CE:** T28, T36, T39, T73, T74, T75, T81, T82, T89, T108, T120, T128; **MI:** T28, T36, T51, T120; **CI:** T28, T37, T44, T66, T97, T135

Tell Jokes and Riddles, PS: T18, T20, T36, T79; **TW:** T61; **MI:** T25, T67

Understand Concepts of Print

Directionality (see Track Print From Left to Right)

Identify Punctuation Marks (Period, Question Mark, Exclamation Mark), PV: T61, T66, T74; **PS:** T20, T23, T69, T112, T123, T131; **TW:** T86, T122, T131; **CE:** T16, T28, T86, T120, T122, T132; **MI:** T66, T69, T86, T122, T132; **CI:** T16, T30, T31, T76, T86, T122, T131, T132, T144

Recognize Letter, Word, Sentence Boundaries, PV: T14, T23, T30, T40, T44, T46, T69, T76, T77, T92, T94, T111, T115, T124, T140; **PS:** T23, T69, T69, T76, T86, T92, T115, T132, T138; **TW:** T23, T30, T40, T46, T69, T76, T86, T92, T132, T138; **CE:** T23, T30, T40, T46, T69, T76, T122, T132, T138; **MI:** T20, T23, T30, T40, T46, T69, T76, T82, T92, T122, T132, T138; **CI:** T20, T23, T30, T40, T46, T69, T76, T82, T86, T92, T115, T122, T132, T138

T131, T136; **MI:** T16, T20, T24, T28, T36, T39, T44, T62, T66, T70, T74, T82, T85, T90, T108, T112, T116, T120, T128, T131, T136; **CI:** T16, T20, T24, T28, T36, T39, T44, T62, T66, T70, T74, T82, T85, T90, T108, T112, T116, T120, T128, T131, T136

Write a Story Innovation, PV: T82, T121; **PS:** T70, T82, T116; **TW:** T28, T70, T74; **CE:** T20, T24, T82, T108, T112, T120, T131; **MI:** T82, T128; **CI:** T16, T66, T128

Write About Information Books, TW: T62; **MI:** T16, T20, T24, T36, T37, T39, T44, T51, T66, T70, T85, T90, T108, T112, T116, T120, T128; **CI:** T20, T24, T39, T82, T90, T108, T116, T131, T136

Write Compound Words, TW: T66

Write Descriptive Words, PV: T20, T39, T90; **PS:** T28, T29, T39, T42, T74, T80, T123; **TW:** T36, T106; **CI:** T44

Write Name, PV: T41, T49, T61, T77, T79, T91, T95, T117

Write Rhyming Sentences/Phrases, PV: T36, T62, T109; **TW:** T90, T133; **CI:** T120

Write Sentences, PV: T120; **PS:** T24, T36, T62, T83, T90, T93; T16, T20, T24, T28, T36, T39, T44, T62, T66, T70, T74, T82, T85, T90, T108, T112, T116, T120, T128, T131, T136; **TW:** T24, T70, T108, T112, T116, T120, T131; **CE:** T16, T24, T74, T90, T116, T136; **MI:** T28, T79, T131, T136; **CI:** T24, T27, T68, T70, T84, T108, T112, T114, T116, T130, T131

Write Verses to a Familiar Song, PV: T36; **CE:** T85; **CI:** T85

Integrated Curriculum Activities

Center Workshops

Alphabet, PV: T17, T33, T63, T79, T95; **PS:** T17, T33, T45, T49, T63, T95, T109, T125, T141; **TW:** T33, T49, T79, T91; **CE:** T63, T79, T125; **MI:** T49, T79, T125; **CI:** T33

Art, PV: T33, T41, T67, T75, T83, T87, T91, T109, T117, T121, T125; **PS:** T17, T21, T25, T29, T37, T41, T49, T63, T67, T71, T75, T83, T87, T109, T113, T117, T121, T129, T141; **TW:** T17, T29, T41, T63, T71, T83, T91, T109, T113, T121, T125, T129, T141; **CE:** T17, T21, T33, T37, T45, T60, T75, T83, T91, T117, T121, T129, T133, T137; **MI:** T17, T21, T29, T37, T41, T63, T67, T83, T91, T113, T117, T129, T133, T141; **CI:** T21, T29, T45, T63, T71, T75, T91, T109, T113, T121

Blocks, PV: T141; **PS:** T41; **TW:** T75; **CI:** T17, T41, T83, T133

Cooking, PV: T109, T121, T137; **PS:** T79; **TW:** T37, T45, T63, T71, T87, T113, T117, T121, T125; **CE:** T45, T95; **MI:** T137

Dramatic Play, PV: T21, T41, T49, T71, T87, T113, T137, T141; **PS:** T75, T79, T125, T129; **TW:** T37, T79, T133; **CE:** T17, T29, T41, T137; **MI:** T67, T91; **CI:** T17, T71, T75, T109, T117, T137

Games, PV: T25, T29, T45, T63, T91, T125; **PS:** T33, T71, T103, T113, T137; **TW:** T45, T95; **CE:** T41, T75, T109, T121, T133; **MI:** T41, T95; **CI:** T49, T79, T95

Health & Fitness, PV: T37; **TW:** T33, T49; **CE:** T125; **MI:** T109; **CI:** T113

Listening, PV: T25, T67, T79, T133; **PS:** T25; **CE:** T33, T113; **MI:** T79; **CI:** T79

Math, PV: T17, T71, T75, T83, T95, T113; **PS:** T21, T29, T87, T121, T137; **TW:** T17, T21, T25, T83, T95, T109, T129, T141; **CE:** T49, T67, T83, T117, T141; **MI:** T45, T75, T87, T125; **CI:** T29, T67, T95, T117, T121

Music & Movement. PS: T95; **TW:** T67, T75; **CE:** T25, T29, T79, T87, T95; **MI:** T33, T63, T71, T129; **CI:** T129

Ongoing Project, CI: T17, T21

Science, PV: T37, T129; **PS:** T37, T45, T67, T91, T117, T133; **TW:** T29, T137; **CE:** T21, T25, T37, T49, T67, T71, T91, T113, T141; **MI:** T21, T25, T29, T33, T45, T83, T113, T117, T121, T133, T137, T141; **CI:** T21, T25, T45, T67, T87, T129

Social Studies, PV: T21, T129; **TW:** T25, T41, T67, T87; **CE:** T87; **MI:** T71; **CI:** T63, T83, T91, T133, T137

Writing, PV: T29, T45, T49, T117, T121, T133; **PS:** T83, T133; **TW:** T41, T117, T133; **CE:** T109; **MI:** T25, T49, T87, T95, T109; **CI:** T25, T33, T41, T49, T87, T125, T141

Connections

Science, **PV:** T82
Social Studies, **CI:** T62

Everyday Literacies

Research and Study Skills

Follow Directions (see Follow Directions under Demonstrate Active Listening Skills)

Graphs, PV: T75, T95, T113; **TW:** T21, T25, T95; **CE:** T66; **CI:** T29

Maps, PS: T71, T85, T87, T134; **MI:** T17; **CI:** T85, T131

Use Parts of a Book, PV: T16, T23, T62, T78, T79, T115, T125; **CI:** T69

Use Reference Sources, PV: T29, T45, T71, T85, T107, T133; **PS:** T14, T33, T37, T45, T63, T99; **TW:** T18, T87, T109; **CI:** T21, T29, T63, T71, T87, T88, T109, T118

Kindergarten Concepts (ALSO SEE Acquiring World Knowledge)

Colors, PS: T23, T25, T32, T39, T41, T49, T66, T86, T94, T121, T124, T131, T133, T137; **TW:** T14, T17, T32, T48, T61, T64, T78, T81, T94, T109, T116, T132, T140, T141; **CE:** T47; **MI:** T67; **CI:** T118

Days, Months, Year on Calendar, PV: T72, T73, T75; **TW:** T18–T20; **CI:** T29, T89

Numbers, PS: T120, T132; **TW:** T129, T132; **CE:** T49; **MI:** T73, T74, T75

Opposites, PV: T43, T45, T65; **PS:** T26, T28, T43; **TW:** T36; **CI:** T64

Positional Relationships, PV: T16, T22, T34, T38, T60, T65, T92; **PS:** T115; **TW:** T35; **CE:** T79; **CI:** T43

Shapes, PS: T18, T21, T23, T137; **TW:** T17, T45, T71, T75, T81, T109, T141; **CE:** T15, T33, T45, T47, T106; **MI:** T21, T26, T29, T65, T67, T75, T141; **CI:** T75

Transportation, PV: T69, T71; **PS:** T85; **CI:** T14, T15, T60, T63, T106, T132

Index

INSTRUCTIONAL ISSUES

Assessment

Ongoing Assessment

Benchmarks, PV: T53, T99, T145; **PS:** T53, T99, T145; **TW:** T53, T99, T145; **CE:** T53, T99, T145; **MI:** T53, T99, T145; **CI:** T53, T99, T145

Comprehension Check, PV: T16, T20, T28, T36, T44, T62, T66, T74, T82, T90, T108, T112, T120, T128, T136; **PS:** T16, T20, T28, T36, T44, T62, T66, T74, T82, T90, T108, T112, T120, T128, T136; **TW:** T16, T20, T28, T36, T44, T62, T66, T74, T82, T90, T108, T112, T120, T128, T136; **CE:** T16, T20, T28, T36, T44, T62, T66, T74, T82, T90, T108, T112, T120, T128, T136; **MI:** T16, T20, T28, T36, T44, T62, T66, T74, T82, T90, T108, T112, T120, T128, T136; **CI:** T16, T20, T28, T36, T44, T62, T66, T74, T82, T90, T108, T112, T120, T128, T136

Observation, PV: T16, T17, T21, T25, T29, T33, T37, T41, T44, T45, T49, T62, T63, T66, T67, T71, T75, T79, T83, T87, T91, T97, T108, T109, T112, T113, T117, T121, T125, T129, T133, T137, T141, T143; **PS:** T17, T20, T21, T25, T33, T37, T41, T44, T45, T49, T50, T63, T66, T67, T71, T75, T79, T83, T87, T91, T95, T97, T109, T112, T113, T117, T121, T125, T129, T133, T137, T141, T143; **TW:** T17, T20, T21, T25, T29, T33, T37, T41, T45, T49, T51, T53, T63, T66, T67, T71, T75, T79, T83, T87, T91, T95, T97, T109, T112, T113, T117, T121, T125, T129, T133, T137, T141, T143; **CE:** T17, T20, T21, T25, T29, T33, T37, T41, T45, T49, T51, T62, T63, T66, T67, T71, T75, T79, T83, T87, T91, T95, T97, T109, T112, T113, T121, T124, T125, T129, T133, T137, T141, T143; **MI:** T17, T20, T21, T25, T29, T33, T37, T41, T45, T49, T51, T63, T66, T67, T71, T75, T79, T83, T87, T91, T95, T97, T109, T113, T117, T121, T125, T129, T133, T137, T141, T143; **CI:** T17, T20, T21, T25, T29, T33, T41, T45, T49, T51, T63, T66, T67, T71, T75, T79, T83, T87, T91, T95, T97, T109, T112, T113, T117, T121, T125, T129, T133, T136, T137, T141, T143

Portfolio

Portfolio Opportunities, PV: T52, T63, T145; **PS:** T52, T63, T145; **TW:** T52, T63, T145; **CE:** T52, T63, T145; **MI:** T52, T63, T145; **CI:** T52, T63, T145

Cultural Connections

Africa, **PS:** T134
African American, **PV:** T35
Celebrations, **TW:** T19
China, **CE:** T131
Family Backgrounds, **PV:** T96
Food, **TW:** T16, T34
France, **CE:** T131; **CI:** T118
Grandparents, **PV:** T66
Japan, **CE:** T127, T128, T131
Maps, **PS:** T134
Other Languages, **PS:** T89

Home/School Connections

PV: T16, T32, T36, T40, T48, T66, T78, T86, T94, T124, T132, T140, T145
PS: T16, T32, T40, T48, T78, T86, T94, T124, T132, T140, T145
TW: T16, T32, T48, T78, T86, T94, T124, T132, T140, T145

CE: T16, T32, T40, T48, T78, T86, T94, T124, T132, T140, T145
MI: T16, T32, T40, T48, T78, T86, T94, T124, T132, T140, T145
CI: T16, T32, T40, T48, T78, T86, T94, T124, T128, T132, T140, T145

Groups

Small Cooperative Groups

PV: T23, T31, T32, T38, T39, T47, T48, T69, T73, T78, T83, T94, T99, T108, T112, T113, T120, T128, T140, T144
PS: T16, T23, T27, T28, T29, T32, T36, T40, T43, T48, T51, T62, T69, T71, T74, T78, T82, T86, T90, T92, T93, T94, T99, T108, T112, T115, T120, T121, T124, T128, T140, T143, T145
TW: T17, T20, T21, T23, T27, T29, T40, T62, T69, T94, T108, T112, T115, T117, T124, T140, T144
CE: T16, T20, T23, T29, T32, T35, T48, T66, T69, T78, T79, T90, T94, T99, T108, T115, T120, T121, T124, T133, T140
MI: T16, T23, T28, T29, T32, T40, T44, T48, T53, T66, T67, T69, T74, T78, T90, T94, T112, T124, T129, T136, T137, T140, T143
CI: T16, T28, T32, T36, T41, T48, T53, T66, T74, T78, T83, T90, T94, T95, T108, T109, T112, T113, T115, T124, T125

Individuals

PV: T40, T117
TW: T87, T91

Partners

PV: T47, T53, T86, T89, T117, T125, T132
PS: T33, T40, T71, T86, T132
TW: T37, T44, T75, T86, T87, T108, T113, T119, T132
CE: T87, T111, T123, T132
MI: T32, T128, T132, T139
CI: T40, T132

Real-Life Connections

Acquiring World Knowledge (ALSO SEE Center Workshops)

Center Workshops
Aa Is For . . ., **PS:** T33
Aa to Zz Pretzels, **CE:** T63
ABC Fun!, **PV:** T79
Act Out *Ii's!*, **TW:** T79
Act Out *Ee's!*, **PS:** T125
Add Another!, **PV:** T125
"All About Me" Cubbies, **PV:** T21
All "Sorts" of Things, **TW:** T21
All We Are, **PV:** T21
Animal Act, **CE:** T17
Animal Close-Up, **MI:** T45
Animal Crackers, **TW:** T45; **CE:** T45

Teacher Resources

Rain, Ice, and Rivers, **CI:** T25
Raining Animals, **PS:** T63
Research Spiders, **CE:** T71
Rhyming Book, A, **TW:** T133
Rock Count, **CE:** T141
Rocks, Rivers, and Rainbows, **CE:** T141
Seasonal Scenes, **CI:** T29
Seeds and Sacks, **MI:** T121
Self-Portrait, **PS:** T83
Sense-able Applesauce, **PV:** T109
Set Up the Claymator's Studio, **PS:** T117
Sew an *Xx* Picture, **MI:** T141
Shadow Animals, **CI:** T117
Shape Up!, **PS:** T137
Shapes in Nature, **MI:** T21
Share a Favorite Story, **PV:** T129
Sing the ABC's, **PV:** T79
Slip, Slither, and Slide, **MI:** T33
Smooth or Scratchy?, **MI:** T49
So Early in the Morning, **MI:** T129
Sort *Aa*'s and *Bb*'s!, **PS:** T17
Sort and Recycle, **CI:** T87
Sort the Steps, **CE:** T133
Sorting by Sound, **PV:** T125
Sounds and Stories, **CE:** T41
Sow a Seed, **MI:** T133
Sponge City, **CI:** T75
Still Life, **PS:** T25
Story Map, **TW:** T83
Story Sketch, **PS:** T129
Strike Up the Band!, **CE:** T29
Sweet, Sour, Salty, **MI:** T33
Taking Root, **TW:** T137
Telephone Talk, **PV:** T49
Tell a Story, **PV:** T33; **TW:** T117
This Land Is Your Land, **CI:** T109
This Little Piggy, **CE:** T75
Time of Day Chart, **CI:** T67
Tissue-Paper Animals, **CI:** T113
Tons of *Tt*'s, **MI:** T49
Touch-and-Feel Chart, **MI:** T71
Toy for Clifford, A, **CE:** T83
Travel Agent, **PV:** T71
Transportation Tally, **PV:** T71
Trash Graph, **TW:** T25
Travel to Anywhere, **CI:** T63
Tree Safari, **MI:** T83
Trim a Birthday Tree, **PV:** T75
Tt Games, **MI:** T49
Up-Down, Under-Over, **MI:** T79
Uppercase and Lowercase Letters, **PV:** T63
Vv Hunt, The, **MI:** T95
Vv Is for Viper!, **MI:** T95
Very Important People, **PV:** T41

Wash and Dry!, **PS:** T91
Watch It Change!, **CE:** T63
Water World, **MI:** T29
We Are Storytellers, **PV:** T133
We Like Books!, **PV:** T113
Weather Dances, **CE:** T87
What's That Sound?, **CE:** T21
Where Do the Animals Live?, **PS:** T117
Who Am I?, **PS:** T25; **MI:** T67
"Whose Tree Is This?," **CI:** T21
Window Sill Vegetable Gardens, **MI:** T137
Word Sort, **CI:** T95
Working Together Mural, **TW:** T41
World of *Ww*'s, A, **MI:** T125
Would You Like to Hear My Story?, **PV:** T133
Writing Sentences, **PS:** T83
X-Ray Vision, **MI:** T141
Zooming, **CE:** T91
Zz Choices, **CI:** T49

Journal Opportunities

PV: T16, T20, T23, T28, T32, T36, T40, T44, T48, T62, T66, T69, T74, T78, T86, T90, T94, T108, T112, T120, T124, T128, T132, T136, T140

PS: T16, T20, T23, T28, T32, T36, T40, T44, T48, T62, T66, T69, T74, T78, T82, T86, T90, T94, T108, T112, T116, T120, T124, T128, T132, T136, T140

TW: T16, T20, T23, T28, T32, T36, T40, T44, T48, T62, T66, T69, T74, T78, T86, T90, T94, T108, T115, T120, T124, T128, T132, T136, T140

CE: T16, T20, T23, T28, T32, T36, T40, T44, T48, T62, T66, T69, T74, T78, T82, T86, T90, T94, T108, T112, T115, T120, T124, T128, T132, T136, T140

MI: T16, T20, T23, T28, T32, T36, T40, T44, T48, T62, T66, T69, T74, T78, T86, T90, T94, T108, T112, T116, T120, T124, T128, T132, T136, T140

CI: T16, T20, T23, T28, T32, T36, T40, T44, T48, T62, T66, T69, T74, T78, T86, T90, T94, T108, T112, T116, T120, T124, T128, T132, T136, T140

Mentors

Chapin, Tom, **CI:** T6, T11, T57, T103
Mora, Pat, **CE:** T6, T11, T57, T103
Powell, Steve, **MI:** T6, T11, T57, T103
Twumasi, Kwaku, **TW:** T6, T11, T57, T103
Wada, Honey, **PV:** T6, T11, T57, T103
Wible, Becky, **PS:** T6, T11, T57, T103

Places

Gardening Center, **MI:** T99
Performance Stage, **CI:** T99
Restaurant, **TW:** T99
Storytelling Corner, **PV:** T99

Projects

"All About You and Me in School," **PV:** T145
"Animals Say Hello" Big Book, **CE:** T43
Big Book of Family Members, **PV:** T99
Big Book of Menus, **TW:** T145
Big Book of Recipes, **TW:** T99

Index

LITERATURE

Genre

ABC Books

A Was Once an Apple Pie, **PV:** T14–T16, T38–T40, T60–T62, T106–T108
ABC Drive, **CI:** T14–T16, T60–T62, T106–T108
Alphabatics, **CE:** T14–T16, T60–T62, T106–T108
Amazon Alphabet, **MI:** T14–T16, T60–T62, T106–T108
Apples, Alligators and Also Alphabets, **PS:** T14–T16, T60–T62, T106–T108
Eating the Alphabet: Fruits and Vegetables from A to Z, **TW:** T14–T16, T60–T62, T106–T108

Concept Books

100th Day of School, The, **TW:** T18–T20, T22–T23
City Sounds, **CI:** T80–T82
From Head to Toe, **MI:** T64–T66, T68–T69
I Like Me!, **PV:** T118–T120
I Went Walking, **PS:** T64–T66, T68–T69
Mice Squeak, We Speak, **MI:** T26–T28
Over on the Farm, **MI:** T72–T74
What Am I?, **PS:** T18–T20, T22–T23

Emergent Readers

My Books

Animal Sounds, **PV:** T140
Banana Bread, **MI:** T32
Empty Box, An, **TW:** T78
Getting Ready, **PS:** T78
Hair, **PS:** T48
I Can Be, **PV:** T32
I Can Draw, **CE:** T124
I Can Too, **PV:** T48
I Read, You Read, **TW:** T140
I Run, **CE:** T78
I Spy!, **MI:** T78
In the Garden, **CI:** T140
In the Nest, **CI:** T78
In the Park, **TW:** T32
It's Playtime!, **CE:** T48
Let's Walk, **MI:** T94
Listen!, **CI:** T48
Little Plant, **MI:** T124
"Meow," Said the Kitten, **CE:** T32
My Family, **PV:** T94
My Name Is Sam, **CE:** T94
Our Snowman, **TW:** T94
Our Town, **CI:** T124
Time to Get Up!, **PS:** T94
Too Small, **MI:** T140
Under Your Feet, **CI:** T94
We Clean Up, **TW:** T48
We Dance, **TW:** T124
We Like Food!, **PV:** T124

We Like to Build, **CE:** T140
Where Did They Go?, **PS:** T124
Where Is My Cat?, **PV:** T78
Who Can Help?, **PS:** T140
Who Is Ben?, **PS:** T32
Who Needs a Tree?, **CI:** T32
Zoo Sense, **MI:** T48

High-Frequency Reader

Band, The, **TW:** T70, T86
Big, **MI:** T116, T132
Can You See It?, **CE:** T70, T86
Dogs, **TW:** T24, T40
I Am, **PS:** T10, T40
I Can See, **PS:** T70, T86
I Like, **PV:** T116, T132
In the Forest, **CI:** T24, T40
Kittens, **PS:** T116, T132
Look!, **MI:** T70, T86
Lunch, **PV:** T70, T86
My Cats, **MI:** T24, T40
School, **PV:** T24, T40
We Are Painting, **TW:** T116, T132
We Can Go!, **CE:** T24, T40
We Like Fruit, **CE:** T116, T132
We Like to Play!, **CI:** T70, T86
What Is It?, **CI:** T116, T132

WiggleWorks Books

Birds on Stage, **PS:** T34–T36
Boots, **PS:** T80–T82
Clifford, The Big Red Dog, **CE:** T80–T82
Let's Get the Rhythm, **CE:** T34–T36
Miss Mary Mack, **PV:** T34–T36
My Garden, **MI:** T126–T127
Pizza, **TW:** T126–T128
Tortillas, **TW:** T34–T36
Tree Can Be, A, **MI:** T80–T82
What Lila Loves, **PV:** T126–T128

Fantasy

Carlos and the Squash Plant, **PS:** T88–T90
Chrysanthemum, **PV:** T26–T28
Clifford, The Big Red Dog, **CE:** T80–T82
Corduroy, **PS:** T118–T120, T143–T144
Cow That Went Oink, The, **TW:** T42–T44
Herman the Helper, **TW:** T26–T28
Minerva Louise at School, **CE:** T118–T120
Mouse Mess, **CE:** T42–T44
Tale of Peter Rabbit, The, **MI:** T134–T136
Where's My Teddy?, **PS:** T42–T44

Fiction

Abuela, **CI:** T72–T74
Blueberries for Sal, **TW:** T118–T120

Index

Credits and Acknowledgments

TEACHER'S EDITION

Acknowledgments

Grateful acknowledgment is made to the following sources for permission to reprint from previously published material. The publisher has made diligent efforts to trace the ownership of all copyrighted material in this volume and believes that all necessary permissions have been secured. If any errors or omissions have inadvertently been made, proper corrections will gladly be made in future editions.

Cover: Ken Bowser for Scholastic Inc.

"Little Black Bug" by Margaret Wise Brown from ANOTHER HERE AND NOW STORYBOOK by Lucy Sprague Mitchell. Copyright © 1937 by E. P. Dutton & Company, Inc. and renewed © 1965 by Lucy Sprague Mitchell. Published by Penguin Putnam Inc.

"Six Little Ducks" from THE FIRESIDE BOOK OF CHILDREN'S SONGS by Marie Winn and Allan Miller. Copyright © 1966 by Marie Winn and Allan Miller. Published by Simon & Schuster.

"The Spider Weaver" from JAPANESE CHILDREN'S FAVORITE STORIES by Florence Sakade. Reprinted by arrangement with Charles E. Tuttle Co., Inc.

"Surprise" © 1985 by Beverly McLoughland was originally published in *Cricket*® magazine, September 1985.

Sentence Strips: Text for sentence strips adapted from LISTEN TO THE DESERT by Pat Mora. Text copyright © 1994 by Pat Mora. Published by arrangement with Clarion Books, a Houghton Mifflin Company imprint.

Book Credits: Cover and spot art from "A-Hunting We Will Go!" from THE FIRESIDE BOOK OF CHILDREN'S SONGS by Marie Winn and Allan Miller. Copyright © 1966 by Marie Winn and Allan Miller. Published by Scholastic Inc., by arrangement with Simon & Schuster. Cover from ALPHABATICS by Suse MacDonald. Copyright © 1986 by Suse MacDonald. Published by Scholastic Inc., by arrangement with Simon & Schuster Books for Young Readers. Cover from CLIFFORD THE BIG RED DOG by Norman Bridwell. Copyright © 1963, 1985 by Norman Bridwell. Published by Scholastic Inc. CLIFFORD and CLIFFORD THE BIG RED DOG are registered trademarks of Norman Bridwell. Cover from GOOD-NIGHT, OWL! by Pat Hutchins. Copyright © 1972 by Pat Hutchins. Published by Scholastic Inc., by arrangement with Simon & Schuster Children's Publishing Division. Cover and spot art from THE ITSY BITSY SPIDER by Iza Trapani. Copyright © 1993 Iza Trapani. Published by Scholastic Inc., by arrangement with Whispering Coyote Press, Inc. Cover from LET'S GET THE RHYTHM, adapted by Anne Miranda, illustrated by Nancy Carpenter. Copyright © 1994 by Scholastic Inc. Published by Scholastic Inc. Cover from LISTEN TO THE DESERT by Pat Mora, illustrated by Francisco X. Mora. Illustrations copyright © 1994 by Francisco X. Mora. Published by Scholastic Inc., by arrangement with Clarion Books, a Houghton Mifflin Company imprint. Cover from MAMA ZOOMS by Jane Cowen-Fletcher. Copyright © 1993 by Jane Cowen-Fletcher. Published by Scholastic Inc. Cover and spot art from MINERVA LOUISE AT SCHOOL by Janet Morgan Stoeke. Copyright © 1996 by Janet Morgan Stoeke. Published by Scholastic Inc., by arrangement with Dutton Children's Books, a division of Penguin Putnam Inc. Cover and spot art from MOUSE MESS by Linnea Riley. Copyright © 1997 by Linnea Riley. Published by The Blue Sky Press, an imprint of Scholastic Inc. Cover and spot art from THE THREE LITTLE PIGS, retold by Gavin Bishop. Copyright © 1989 by Gavin Bishop. Published by Scholastic Inc., by arrangement with Ashton Scholastic, Ltd. Cover and spot art from WHISTLE FOR WILLIE by Ezra Jack Keats. Copyright © 1964 by Ezra Jack Keats. Published by Scholastic Inc., by arrangement with Puffin Books, a division of Penguin Putnam Inc.

Photography and Illustration Credits

Photos: Photo Stylists: Gayna Hoffman, Shawna Johnston. p. T14: Randy Rodriguez for Scholastic Inc. p. T17: Ana Esperenza Nance for Scholastic Inc. Clara Von Aich for Scholastic Inc. p. T18: Clara Von Aich for Scholastic Inc. p. T19: Alan G. Nelson for Scholastic Inc. p. T21: Clara Von Aich for Scholastic Inc. p. T24: Ana Esperanza Nance for Scholastic Inc. p. T25: Clara Von Aich for Scholastic Inc. p. T26: Clara Von Aich for Scholastic Inc. p. T29: David Mager for Scholastic Inc. Ken O'Donoghue for Scholastic Inc. p. T32: Joan Baron for Scholastic Inc. p. T33: Clara Von Aich for Scholastic Inc. p. T35: Clara Von Aich for Scholastic Inc. p. T37: Clara Von Aich for Scholastic Inc. p. T39: Clara Von Aich for Scholastic Inc. p. T40: David Mager for Scholastic Inc. p. T41: Ana Experience Nance for Scholastic Inc. Clara Von Aich for Scholastic Inc. p. T43: Francis Clark Westfield for Scholastic Inc. p. T44: Ana Esperanza Nance for Scholastic Inc. p. T48: David Mager for Scholastic Inc. p. T49: Clara Von Aich for Scholastic Inc. p. T50: Clara Von Aich for Scholastic Inc. p. T52: Ana Esperanaza Nance for Scholastic Inc. Randy Roderiguez for Scholastic Inc. p. T62: David Mager for Scholastic Inc. p. T63: Clara Von Aich for Scholastic Inc. David Mager for Scholastic Inc. p. T64: Clara Von Aich for Scholastic Inc. p. T67: Ana Esperanza Nance for Scholastic Inc. Bie Bostrom for Scholastic Inc. p. T71: Ken O'Donoghue for Scholastic Inc. p. T73: Clara Von Aich for Scholastic Inc. p. T74: Clara Von Aich for Scholastic Inc. p. T75: Clara Von Aich for Scholastic Inc. p. T79: Clara Von Aich for Scholastic Inc. p. T80: Bie Bostrom for Scholastic Inc. p. T82: Ana Esperanza Nance for Scholastic Inc. Clara Von Aich for Scholastic Inc. p. T83: Ana Esperanza Nance for Scholastic Inc. © Dogue Allemand/Animals, Animals. p. T86: David Mager for Scholastic Inc. p. T87: Clara Von Aich for Scholastic Inc. p. T88: Clara Von Aich for Scholastic Inc. p. T89: David Mager for Scholastic Inc. p. T90: Clara Von Aich for Scholastic Inc. p. T91: Clara Von Aich for Scholastic Inc. p. T94: Ana Seperanaza Nance for Scholastic Inc. Clara Von Aich for Scholastic Inc. p. T95: Clara Von Aich for Scholastic Inc. p. T96: Ana Seperanaza Nance for Scholastic Inc. p. T99: Clara Von Aich for Scholastic Inc. p. T108: Francis Clark Westfield for Scholastic Inc. p. T109: Clara Von Aich for Scholastic Inc. p. T110: © Richard Kolar/Animals, Animals. p. T112: John Chellman for Scholastic Inc.

p. T113: Clara Von Aich for Scholastic Inc. p. T116: David Lawrence for Scholastic Inc. p. T117: Clara Von Aich for Scholastic Inc. p. T120: Clara Von Aich for Scholastic Inc. p. T121: Clara Von Aich for Scholastic Inc. p. T124: David Mager for Scholastic Inc. p. T125: Clara Von Aich for Scholastic Inc. p. T132: David Mager for Scholastic Inc. p. T133: Clara Von Aich for Scholastic Inc. p. T134: Clara Von Aich for Scholastic Inc. Leah Margulies for Scholastic Inc. p. T137: Clara Von Aich for Scholastic Inc. David Mager for Scholastic Inc. p. T140: Clara Von Aich for Scholastic Inc. David Mager for Scholastic Inc. p. T141: Clara Von Aich for Scholastic Inc. p. T142: Clara Von Aich for Scholastic Inc. p. T145: Francis Clark Westfield for Scholastic Inc.

Upfront pages: All reduced facsimiles of Student Anthologies, Teacher's Editions, ancillary components, and interior pages are credited, if necessary, in their original publication format.

Illustrations: p. T45: Gayna Hoffman for Scholastic Inc. p. T106: Gayna Hoffman for Scholastic Inc. p. T144: Gayna Hoffman for Scholastic Inc.

a b c d

e f g h

i j k l

m n o p

q r s t

u v w x

y z a e

i o u small letters

Name

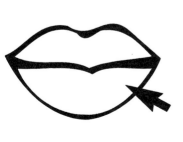

Copyright © Scholastic Inc.

Teacher Note: The above picture cards are: bat, bee, bus, cat, coat, cup, dog, duck, fan, fish, fox, leaf, lip, log, man, moon.

Teacher Note: The above picture cards are: mop, nest, nose, nut, pan, pen, pig, ring, rock, run, six, sock, sun, ten, tie, top.